CAN'T GET THROUGH

THROUGH
8 Barriers to Communication

CAN'T GET THROUGH

8 Barriers to Communication

Kevin Hogan, Psy.D.
Ron Stubbs, C.I.

PELICAN PUBLISHING COMPANY
Gretna 2003

*The word "Pelican and the depiction of a pelican are trademarks
of Pelican Publishing Company, Inc., and are
registered in the U.S. Patent and Trademark Office.*

Library of Congress Cataloging-in-Publication Data

Hogan, Kevin.
  Can't get through : eight barriers to communication / Kevin
Hogan, Ron Stubbs.
    p. cm.
  Includes bibliographical references (p.   ).
  ISBN 1-58980-075-3
  1. Interpersonal communication. I. Stubbs, Ron. II. Title.

BF637.C45 H635 2003
153.6—dc21
                        2003002790

Printed in the United States of America

Published by Pelican Publishing Company, Inc.
1000 Burmaster Street, Gretna, Louisiana 70053

For Jessica and Mark,
The kids that make my wheels turn.

To my beautiful wife and best friend, Jeanie.
You never stopped believing in me.

To Heather and Mackenzie.
You both hold the strings to my heart.

Contents

CONTENTS

Acknowledgments

Both of us would like to thank Nina Kooij and Dr. Milburn Calhoun for making this project happen. We also want to say thank you to Joseph Billingsley, the sales manager at Pelican, and Rachel Carner, my publicist. You guys are the greatest. Special thanks to Jim Calhoun, the project editor.

From Kevin:

To Dena Moscola, Joe Duchene, Devin and Rachel Hastings, Katherin Scott, Terry Watts, Bev Bryant, Rebecca Cahill, Elsom Eldridge, and Meredith Kaplan. And of course to Jessica and Mark Hogan . . . the kids that make my wheels turn . . . and Katie Hogan, the greatest mom in the world.

A special thanks to my collaborator, Ron Stubbs. Thanks for sharing your wisdom and expertise!

From Ron:

Thank you to my family, Jeanie, Heather, and Mac, for

all their support, encouragement, and love when Dad was locked away in the office writing this book. You three keep me sane.

To my parents, Jim and Edie Stubbs. Bet you never expected this, did you? I love you both.

To Rolf and Pat Flaten. You are like second parents to me. Thanks for letting into your hearts.

To Marshall and KaZ. Thanks for keeping me company in the middle of the night and keeping my feet warm.

And most of all, to my mentor, my soul brother, my friend, Kevin Hogan, for believing in me enough to offer me this chance. Thank you.

Introduction

It's always difficult to distill something as important and complex as human communication into a few categories of importance. Then it's even more demanding to discuss the barriers to effective communication in a simple, rapid-fire fashion that is easy to read and implement. It's my belief that you will be able to improve the communication you participate in to such an extent that it will actually change your life. That's my goal. I believe it is attainable.

Having observed thousands of people communicate as a therapist for many years, I have discovered that there are eight general ways that people lose the attention and respect of others when communicating. Having trained in the corporate world for the past seven years, I have seen these same elements abused over and over again. This book will help the person in business and in their personal relationships.

What are the eight barriers to communication that have the world stumped?

1. Failure to Make a Great First (and Second) Impression

2. Flubbing the Story
3. Not Listening
4. Arguing with the Intent to Harm
5. Criticism
6. Hostility and Contempt
7. Ignoring Body Language
8. Ignoring the Cycle of Communication

Have you ever been in a conversation where you found your mind drifting, dreaming, and struggling to stay focused? Do you remember how it feels to listen as someone drones on and on? When we are faced with a poor communicator there can be many reasons for the missed connection. Often there are words and phrases that simply shut us down and prevent us from listening as well as we would like.

Many times the person communicating is injecting so many negative words and ideas that we begin to feel down and heavy inside. It may just be that the person you are communicating with is boring you because the content of the communication is all about them, about stories you don't care to listen to, and people you have never met!

What if that poor communicator who is boring someone to tears . . . is you? How would you know if you are the one who is inserting negative associations, bringing up insignificant details, droning on about you, you, you? How do you know if someone is really interested in what you have to say . . . that they are really engaged in the conversation? What is your method of observing whether or not the person or group is interested and intrigued, or tired and looking for the door?

When you become a top-notch communicator, you learn from everyone you talk with. You will notice the subtle cues that tell you if you have good rapport, speaking in a way that your audience understands and using words that create desire and interest. You will be willing to identify in yourself those things that push others away and prevent them from listening as well as you would like. This is a very potent aspect of self-awareness that allows you to stay fascinating to everyone around you!

Throughout this book you will look at the areas of communication where people most often go wrong. You will discover how you may have been alienating others and helping them to feel negative when they are around you. As you read these scenarios, notice if you see yourself in them. Take time to be very honest about your style of communication and the effects you are having on those around you.

I've asked my colleague and friend Ron Stubbs to contribute to this book in areas where he is an expert. Ron is a psychotherapist specializing in hypnosis. I've seen some of the cards that Ron has received over the years. They say things like "Thank you for saving my life."

Ron has learned how to communicate complex ideas in a very easy to understand fashion, and I've asked him to share his expertise about listening, criticism, and the cycle of effective communication. This book is a better tool for you because of Ron's contribution.

Enough accolades. Let's get to it!

Kevin Hogan
Minneapolis
January 2003

Chapter One

Failure to Make a Great First (and Second) Impression

The best place to begin this book is . . . at the beginning. You can't do much to change anything that you have communicated in the past. The future is a different story. You can literally mold yourself into one of the finest communicators on the planet if you follow the suggestions in overcoming the eight barriers to communication. Throughout this book you will discover how to adopt the skills you are going to learn to business and personal relationships, as most are interchangeable.

There are several facets of communication, many of which people never consider. Here are the most important:

1) You, your beliefs, your intentions, your verbal skills, your empathy.
2) The other person, his/her beliefs, intentions, verbal skills, and empathy.
3) The physical environment (church, football game, school, office).
4) The physical appearance of each communicator.

5) The nonverbal communication of each communicator.
6) The degree to which two people like each other.
7) Gender differences in perception and communication.

In the initial moments after meeting someone, we are judged in a positive or negative light. In these first moments, the unconscious mind is rapidly making determinations of whether or not this person is worth communicating with on any and every level.

The second moments come after the initial contact and saying "hello." If what happens next is taking place at a dance club, the experience will be very different from what we will be talking about in this chapter. Anytime you are in a specialized environment, whether a dance club, a church social, a baseball game, a convention, or a Las Vegas showroom, you have an advantage in "first contact."

In situations such as these you can meet people and talk with them about everything that is happening all around you. Meeting people and having them find you interesting in these specialized environments is enhanced because there are usually a lot of people and they all have the common interest of "being there." Everyone sees everyone else as a little bit more like they are, increasing the "face value" of everyone at the event, even if it is a small increase.

Making a good second impression is a bit more difficult in non-specialized environments. In a restaurant, for example, the activities are not quite so exciting and unifying. In these settings you need to be a little more adept at putting your best foot forward.

Women and men, on average, have certain preferences in communication styles. For several years I have been researching the nuances of the first public meeting between two people. Men and women report some preferences as being similar and others as strikingly different in these first meetings.

Both men and women are influenced by the physical appearance of people when they first meet. One recent study revealed that on blind dates, both men and women would be interested to some degree in another date with a physically attractive person. Both men and women on the blind dates said they would be less interested in dating someone that was not physically attractive in their mind.

When developing rapport, it certainly is important to look as good as you can. We discuss this at length elsewhere in this book. Beyond physical appearance, we have learned that precisely where you sit or stand seems to impact how you are perceived.

In research I have done, men reveal that, on average, they are more comfortable when a woman is seated at a right angle to the man and not directly across from the man. Why this is the case is unclear. It is possible that men like to be in control of an environment and prefer to have a clear view of what is ahead.

Women, on the other hand, say they prefer a man to sit directly across from them in contrast to having him sit beside them or at a right angle! This contradiction in seating and standing preferences is one possible explanation for the difficulties men and women have in first-contact situations.

In addition to this fascinating contrast in preference

style of positioning, men and women (typically right-handed) who converse with people directly in front of them almost universally prefer that person to stand or sit slightly to their right side rather than to their left side. In other words, people prefer to communicate with each other when their right eyes are in alignment, and not their left eyes.

It's possible that this is true because of left-brain/right-brain phenomena.

It seems that the left brain is typically more dominant in language, rational communication, and mathematics. It appears that the right brain is more immature, emotional, and volatile than the left. When looking through one eye or the other, we are connecting with the opposite brain hemisphere.

There are six basic emotions that are identifiable: Fear, anger, sadness, disgust, interest, and happiness. It is possible that when we first meet someone we tend to be uncomfortable. It's also possible that that discomfort may somehow relate to, or trigger, negative emotions that may tend to be more of a right-brain phenomenon.

If this is indeed true, then when we look to our left, we will access more right-brain activity than left and enhance the chances of coming in touch with those more volatile and emotional experiences in memory. Could this be why people report more comfort when someone is seated to their right-hand side? It certainly hasn't been proven but the evidence mounts!

Therefore, when you meet someone new, you may want to play the percentages and meet people so they respond to you in the most favorable light possible. This means that when you are meeting someone, you can shake his/her hand (or participate in whatever greeting is appropriate to the occasion) and then keep that person to your right as you maintain eye contact with them.

Allow yourselves to be seated so that your right eyes are directly opposite each other. This may just give you both a slightly more comfortable feeling than you would have in a different setting.

It's interesting to note that in public demonstrations of this phenomenon, people who sit to the left of another person tend to describe the first emotion that comes to mind as "fear" or "anger." When people sit to the right of another person, they tend to describe their first emotion felt as "fine," "glad to see you," or "happy." The results do not prove the causality, but the evidence is strong. This leads me to believe that your best first impression comes when the other person is seated to your right!

What if the other person is left-handed?

It seems that about 70 percent of left-handers respond as most right-handers do. The other 30 percent seem to be indifferent or prefer the exact opposite preferences we have been discussing.

If all of this seems awfully technical and a lot to remember, just keep in mind that **right eyes lining up makes everything all right.**

MIRRORING

There you are. There they are. You are seated across from each other. The right eyes line up. Now what?

We all tend to like people who are like ourselves. From a physiological perspective, this means that the best impression you can make on other people is probably to emulate their physiology, their posture, and even some of their nonverbal mannerisms.

When you are in that first contact situation you can easily notice how the other person is seated and then model his/her physiology. This is done by adopting a similar body posture and seeing to it that your hand and leg positions are similar. In other words, simply sit as if they were looking in a mirror and seeing themselves. You will find this easy to do.

This process of mirroring another person is often called "matching" or "pacing." When people begin to use similar gestures and experience similar facial responses, they tend to synchronize in other ways that are almost magical. This mirroring can lead to rapport being developed more quickly and sometimes instantly.

LEADING

It can be very useful in communication to know if your belief that you are synchronized with another person is correct. One strategy that you can use is to briefly stop mirroring the persons you are with and do something different. (Take a drink from a glass of water, move forward, smile, etc.) See if they move out of the position that they were in. If they do, you probably are synchronized with the other person and are, indeed, in rapport. The other person doesn't have to match your exact behavior. You simply want to know if they move in some way.

If not, continue pacing (mirroring) until they will accept your lead into a different physiology.

The nonverbal dance of pacing and leading is one

that will come with practice and when you have become more comfortable in first-contact situations.

PACING AND LEADING WITH YOUR VOICE

The dance goes beyond nonverbal communication. (Nonverbal communication will be discussed in greater detail later in the book!)

Have you noticed that people speak at different rates? Do you feel comfortable with people who speak at a very different rate than yourself? Most people don't. Imagine for just a moment that two people are having dinner and one of them is speaking at a mile a minute. Words flow from his/her mouth like water from a fire hydrant.

The other person, on the other hand, speaks as if there is a tightly woven coffee filter in his/her mouth, slowing the pace of their communication to a virtual standstill. These two people are not likely to build rapport with each other. They process and articulate information in a different fashion from each other.

It is generally easier for people who normally speak quickly to slow down than it is for people who speak slowly to speak more quickly. People who speak quickly normally perceive slower communicators to be dull and boring on the negative side and gentle and caring on the positive side. The fast-paced communicator often becomes impatient with the pace of the slower communicator.

People who speak slowly consider those who speak quickly to be aggressive and often rude on the negative side. Positive attributes ascribed to the fast-paced communicator include intelligence and quick thinking.

We believe there are approximately three different speeds at which people communicate. Each of these speeds will change throughout a conversation, depending upon the content of the conversation. Depending on a person's default speaking pace and mood, that person will speak in one of three ranges of pace: fast-paced, moderate-paced, and slow-paced.

People who speak quickly are generally visually oriented and speak as quickly as they see the pictures in their minds. Medium-paced communicators seem to be very auditory in nature. In other words, they tend to speak in such a manner that points to the quality of the words they say. They may hear their own voice more clearly than other people. They may have a greater awareness of the affect their voice has on other people.

Finally, the emotional communicator is the person who tends to speak more slowly. They seem to sort their thoughts through their emotions. They might be more sensitive to people and therefore careful about what they say.

If you can pace the other person's speaking style in a first contact meeting, your partner will see you in a more positive light. As was noted earlier, it is easier to slow down in communication than it is to speed up! Regardless, moving your "speed control" in the general direction of your first-contact partner will enhance their impressions of you as to being more like them. This increases rapport and makes everything that happens for the rest of the meeting more likely to succeed.

We all tend to evaluate other people by the sound of their voice, the words they choose to communicate with, their tonality, and especially their pacing. Until you become unconsciously adept at matching another person's vocal pacing, consciously alter your own speaking habits so that they more closely match those around you.

How can you increase your pacing if you are an emotional communicator?

As we noted earlier, increasing your pace is more difficult than reducing your pace!

It is difficult but doable. Begin practicing by reading a page from a book at your regular pace. Count how many words per minute you speak. Now, read the page again into a tape recorder and be certain to articulate all the words clearly as you speak more quickly. Do it again and see if you can talk just a little more quickly, maybe adding twenty words per minute.

The idea is not to race through the page but to learn how to communicate more quickly. About one-third of all communicators are fast-paced, visual speakers. They will perceive you as more credible if you can speak at their level, or at least a bit more swiftly.

THE MISTAKE OF BEING BORING

Have you ever been around someone who just talked and talked and talked and talked and . . . well . . . you get the idea! They droned on forever without ever coming to the point . . . or any point. Now, is it possible that this person was once you? We've all bored other people at one time or another. At a first-contact meeting, we don't have the luxury of doing this! Therefore, here is an exercise that will help you kick the "I can be boring blues!"

Do this exercise when you are alone:

1) Think about a book, movie, or television show that you recently read or saw.

2) Take two minutes to describe the show or book aloud.

3) Pause, compose your thoughts, and then do the same thing again in one minute!

4) Pause, compose your thoughts, and do your review in thirty seconds!!

The ability to be brief and offer a *Reader's Digest* condensed version of any story, especially your personal stories, can be the most profound communication change you may ever make. By making your stories shorter, you give the listeners the opportunity to have you elaborate on what you have just shared with them. If they don't ask for more, you may have just offered the right amount of information!

People who tell long stories while the rest of the group experiences eye-glaze are never perceived as attractive and are avoided. This simple exercise, done regularly, makes you instantly more attractive!

WHAT DO I TALK ABOUT?

First-contact situations tend to be a bit uncomfortable because you are now seated across from someone who you don't know that much about.

The good news is that you don't know anything about this person. That really IS good news. You can explore every avenue and have a lifetime of stories behind every door. The opportunities are fraught with risks, of course. You could easily open a door for which the information you receive will be uncomfortable for one or both of you.

Most people ask about a person's job. That can be a good thing. Most everyone has a job. Research has shown that self-esteem is directly correlated to job satisfaction. If your first-contact partner appears to have great self-esteem, this is a great place to go. But do most people like their jobs? I don't know. You can ask about their family but are most people happy with the relationships in their family? Maybe, but families and the events that happen within a family are a leading cause of distress to most people.

Therefore I like to direct the conversation just a bit.

Talking about the future can be nice but there are problems with the future, too. What if you find out a person is 45 years old and has decided that he has just spent twenty years in the wrong career. He doesn't want to go back to school, he has kids to take care of, and he feels stuck! The future may look more like the past. I avoid the future until a little later.

There are some directions that you can take that are almost fail-safe, however. How do you like this?

> *"So, the end of the week comes. If money were no object, how would you like to spend your days off?"*

It seems to me that most people enjoy having an occasional day off. It also seems to me that most people would like talking about something that they can do if money is no object. I also learn a great deal about a person if I know what he or she would do with their time off. It tells me about what is really important to them in their life.

SELF-DISCLOSURE: BEING VULNERABLE, NOT UNBEARABLE

What is the right mix of conversation? How do you know what to talk about, what not to talk about, and how much? What kind of conversation is most likely to enhance your level of charisma and bring out your best you?

People want to discover what the person they are interested in communicating with is really like inside. Leave negativity behind at your first meeting with someone and save it for later. Much later!

Self-disclosure means that you are going to share some of who you are with another person. Being vulnerable means that you can share a weakness or two, but not necessarily weaknesses that are perceived as negative. You can be a bit self-effacing when communicating with your new friend or associate. This self-disclosure makes your communication more real. You've now disclosed that you are not perfect and have given some of your positive attributes. First-contact partners generally perceive this experience as positive. How might this conversation take place if I was speaking to a first-contact partner?

For the balance of this chapter I'm going to assume we are talking about social relationships, but the methodology for building business relationships is the same.

Kevin: *"Nice to meet you. I'm glad you could have lunch today."*
FCP: *"Thanks. This is a very nice place."*
Kevin: *"Have you ever been here?"*
FCP: *"Never. Have you?"*

Kevin: *"A couple of times. I think you'll like it. When you go out, where do you like to go?"*

FCP: *"You mean restaurants?"*

Kevin: *"In general. Restaurants, movies, entertainment . . . ."*

FCP: *"Hmmm . . . I guess I like just about everything. I like to go to movies. I like to dance, and I like to take walks around the lake."*

Kevin: *"What have you seen lately that you liked at the movies?"*

FCP: *"I thought the new Harry Potter movie was great. Did you see that?"*

Kevin: *"No, I heard it was great. Without giving the ending away, what was it about?"*

FCP: *"Well, let's see. It had the same kids and cast as the first one. The movie followed the book pretty closely and was really pretty magical."*

Kevin: *"Thumbs up or down?"*

FCP: *"Definitely a thumbs up."*

Kevin: *"OK, I'll give you another chance to play movie critic. What other movie have you seen lately that you thought was great?"*

FCP: *"The new* Star Trek *movie."*

Kevin: *"That I saw."*

FCP: *"I thought it was great."*

Kevin: *"Me, too. So, that's two thumbs up."* (smiles) (waiter arrives)

Waiter: *"Would you like to order now?"*

Kevin: *"Not yet. Can we have just a couple of minutes?"*

Waiter: *"Certainly."*

Kevin: *"Some of the dishes are excellent. What kind of food do you like?"*

FCP: *"I like just about everything. I'm pretty easy to please. What about you?"*

Kevin: *"I'm a little more difficult to please than you are, which is why I wanted to meet you here. I don't eat most kinds of seafood, but the chicken, steak, and pastas here are great."*

FCP: *"You don't like seafood?"*

Kevin: *"I was raised in a family that ate a very Jewish-like diet. I still don't eat some things, like crab and lobster. Some of my friends say I missed the boat. I tell them, it was a deep-sea fishing boat and I wasn't allowed to get on in the first place!"*

FCP: (smiles) *"Do you recommend anything?"*

Kevin: *"The Chicken Milano is pretty good if you don't like spicy food. If you do, you might want to . . ."*

And so it goes. The first-contact partner and I are rolling right along. I disclose a little bit about myself, and that will encourage the first-contact partner to feel more open to disclose more about herself later on. There are numerous ways to deal with first contact. Wherever the other person leads you is where you want to go with conversation. Remember, everything is new in first contact so you have a wealth of life experiences to go to. The key is keep it positive.

What might a conversation be like that is not so effective in building rapport? Let's use the same scenario and just change the conversation a bit. Let's see how these people can ruin the first contact:

Kevin: *"Nice to meet you. I'm glad you could have lunch today."*

FCP: *"Thanks, it's a very nice place."*

Kevin: *"Have you ever been here?"*

FCP: *"Never, have you?"*

Kevin: *"A few times. The food is great."* (Never promise something you can't deliver.) *"Don't you just love steakhouses?"* (Don't guess what they might like. Ask them their preferences instead!)

FCP: *"Not really, I'm more of a seafood fan."*

Kevin: *"I don't eat seafood. I used to be a Seventh Day Adventist and it's just sort of stuck over the years."* (The church down the street from yours is probably a cult in someone else's mind, so leave the brand off the building!)

FCP: *"Isn't that a cult?"*

Kevin: *"No, just a conservative church. They eat a Jewish diet, pretty much."*

FCP: *"Huh?"*

Kevin: *"Hey, did you see* Lord of the Rings?"

FCP: *"Yeah."*

Kevin: *"Great movie, wasn't it? Most incredible fantasy movie I've ever seen."*

FCP: *"I thought it was gross."* (Time to skip this, Kevin, and go somewhere else.)

Kevin: *"Well, sure, that was part of the point, right? It was in part a war movie."*

FCP: *"My idea of a fantasy is* You've Got Mail *with Tom Hanks and Meg Ryan."*

Kevin: *"Yeah, that was a good show, too."* (Why didn't you ask her what she liked best about it? Then you learn something about her and what she likes!)

FCP: *"Very romantic."*

Are these two people in sync? No. The reason is that neither of them is eliciting preferences of the other person. Instead, they are making statements about their personal experience without thought of how the other person might feel about them. Too much disclosure too fast, and it isn't even significant disclosure. Each of these two people is in his or her own little world, and neither is interested in penetrating the other person's reality!

The differences are subtle but make all the difference in the world in the rapport-building process. This conversation is uncomfortable and going nowhere.

It's hard to be interested in someone who can only start a sentence with the word "I." People who are irresistible are those people who are able to make other people feel important and cared about. When you start too many sentences with the word "I," the message is clear . . . you are interested in yourself. What follows are common mistakes people make in communicating, followed by the better way to express the thought, maximizing one's irresistibility:

Mistake: *"I really like football. I'm a big Vikings fan."*
Better: *"Do you like sports?"*

(Wait for the response before delving any further. If you get a negative response you've saved the person the struggle of being bored at a first meeting.)

Mistake: *"I come here all the time."*
Better: *"Have you ever been here before?"*

(So, you bring all the guys/girls here. That makes me feel really special. Thanks for making me just one of the many instead of making first contact something special.)

Mistake: *"I just bought a '69 Chevy."*

(When was the last time you met a woman who knew the difference between a '69 and a '79, or even cared? They are out there, but only at the car rallies.)

Mistake: *"My old boyfriend used to take me here."*
Better: *"Yes, I've been here before. I really like it. I'm glad you chose it."*

(No man on earth is interested in your past boyfriends or husbands. If the earth quakes and he happens to ask about former times and loves, touch on them and leave the subject. These are areas you should leave alone in first contact.)

Mistake: *"You have a beautiful body."*
Better: *"I really like your hair."*

(First contact is no time to be talking about her body. Your eyes should be focused from the neck up. Leave the rest for another day.)

Mistake: *"I love Mariah Carey."*
Better: *"Who is your favorite recording artist?"*

(Ask whom they find exciting first and see what it is about that performer that they like. Then share your interests.)

All of these simple but important changes in the way we communicate make us appear to be fascinating because we are focusing on the other person first. We can talk about our interests later. Learn what you can about the person you are with. The idea is not to agree that you like Mariah Carey if you don't, but to learn about the interests and loves of your first-contact partner. You can detail why Tina Turner is your favorite female entertainer at a later date. Find out what they like and you can make your second meeting custom-made especially for your first contact partner.

Can't I tell them anything about me?

You can and you must participate in mutual self-disclosure so your first-contact partner can learn about you as well. If you are too mysterious, then they will ultimately lose interest in you. However, most people aren't too mysterious. Most people are too talkative. Once on a roll people tend to disclose far too much far too quickly. Even if your bank account has seven digits, she probably doesn't want to know yet. She'd probably like to figure it out over a few dates.

The best policy is to always put your attention on the other person, his/her interests, likes, and dislikes. When you are asked about your specific likes and dislikes, you should always be frank and upfront. However, all things considered, participate in less "I" and more "you." People will find you more interesting to talk with!

When you are in a position of disclosure, you should focus toward the positive. She may ask whether you like your job. You probably hate your job. You can't lie. You can be just a bit evasive, a bit optimistic, and put your best foot forward.

Here are some examples: Your first-contact partner asks you the following questions. Your first response right below the question is of course true, but bluntly honest. In the second response you are honest, optimistic, and put everything into a positive light.

"Do you like children?"

Poor: *"Kids drive me nuts."* (She probably has one, don't you think?)

Better: *"Isn't everyone a child inside?"*

"Do you like your job?"

Poor: *"No, I can't wait to leave."* (sign of instability.)

Better: *"You know, I've been there three years. I have learned so much about the structure of companies. I can see myself there for three more years or maybe even finding something that would be even more fun and exciting. How about you?"*

"Do you like wrestling?"

Poor: *"It's a stupid form of entertainment."* (Her brother is a wrestler, right? Who did you just insult that is related to her?)

Better: *"I've never been to a wrestling match. Have you?"*

"Who are you voting for in the election?"

Poor: *"Straight Democratic ticket."* (50-50 chance you just offended him.)

Better: *"I need to know just a little more about the candidates. I like a lot about several of the candidates. How about you?"*

"What do you think about the company's decision to lay off 2,000 workers?"

Poor: *"They got laid off because they weren't producing enough income to justify their salary."* (Read that to mean your brother is a loser.)

Better: *"My hope is that people will find something that makes them happy and excited about their lives. It's always frustrating when people lose their jobs, but I bet you can remember times when people have told you it turned out to be the best thing that ever could have happened. You know what I mean?"*

"Where do you stand on the abortion issue?"

Poor: Any response. (Deadly question if the two of you disagree.)

Better: Smile and say, *"Wow, now I know how a presidential candidate feels. That is a really hard question to answer. You sit in front of someone you think is really incredible and you wouldn't do anything to offend them in any way. I think I would do whatever it would take to not answer the question. At least not tonight."*

In each situation, you could have said exactly what you think. Unfortunately, in every case noted on the previous pages, that would have potentially polarized you from your first-contact partner. The "better" responses are all respectful, optimistic, and allow for a slower disclosure.

They may think that it is completely reasonable to ask each of these questions, but few people think about what happens if you completely disagree on something that is significant to them. Therefore you need to be aware that a positive and optimistic response that allows for eventual and not immediate disclosure can be very wise.

This is particularly true in discussing your current job. No one wants to hear that a person (especially a man) hates his job. It indicates general instability. Instability is not a bad word. It simply means, "not stable." Women, in particular, are looking for stability in their relationships with both men and women. The time to disclose all feelings about a job is probably not at first contact. You never have to lie about your true feelings and, in fact, you should never lie, but this is a good time to find something positive to say and put a good light on something you have negative feelings about.

There is so much you can do to make your first and second impressions a success. Doing so primes the pump for further success in communication. Underestimating the power of the first and second contact with someone is a big mistake.

You already have figured out that everything that is important in the first and second impression is important in all of your communications. Next you will learn how to share the threads of your life with those you want to talk to!

Chapter Two

Flubbing the Story

Most conversations include at least one story. Some longer conversations include two dozen or more stories! When you tell someone a story, it's really important to you that the person you are talking to listens. It makes you feel good when they "oooooh" and "ahhhh-hh." When people gloss over your stories, you feel let down and sometimes hurt. Our stories are important to us and we want them to be important to others.

Everything you have become today is part of your life story, the sum of all of your stories about your life. It means the world to you when people are fascinated by your stories.

Remember when the little Texas girl Jessica McClure fell in the well and was trapped? It took three days to get her out. The nation watched. Would she live or die? Could the rescuers get to her in time? That happened in 1987. You don't even know Jessica but you probably remember it to this day! Each year millions of people die and experience incredible events. The story of Jessica was a great story and it unfolded right before our eyes.

The media calls these kinds of stories "human interest" stories. They sell news shows because people are engaged by the drama. Each of us has at least one human interest story to tell about ourselves. A time when you survived something dramatic. You overcame an illness. You persisted until you succeeded. You helped someone in great need, and someone found out about it and told someone else who told the news and then *you* made the news. All of these are great stories.

Telling stories well and listening to them with fascination are two important factors in maintaining good communication. You'd think it would be easy to tell and listen to stories but this isn't the case. "Flubbing the story" is the first of the mistakes we make when communicating.

There are ten ways to flub a story.

1) Be boring.

2) Talk too long.

3) Speak too slowly.

4) Speak in a garbled way so that people can't understand you.

5) Exaggerate when telling your story.

6) Ignore feedback during your storytelling.

7) Respond to other people's stories with a story of your own.

8) Poke holes in other people's special stories.

9) Overtly brag about yourself just a little too much.

10) Not telling your stories with intention.

Let's look at each of these ten ways to flub a story and then talk about how to tell a story so people will listen, be fascinated, and be asking for more!

1) **Be boring.**

Being boring centers around being focused on yourself. Even when telling stories you must be paying attention to the persons listening to you. You must think ahead of time, "Why do they want to hear this story?" "How can I tell this story so it is interesting to them?" Your stories will usually be about your experiences. How you tell your stories and how you position yourself in your stories will determine just how interested the other person will be.

2) **Talk for too long.**

If you are in an everyday conversation, you probably have less than one minute to tell your story. Learn to tell what I call a "thumbnail" or a *"Readers Digest* condensed version" of your story.

I remember when my sister was a pre-teen she would come home from the movies and recite virtually all the lines of the movie line for line, scene for scene. My eyes would glaze over by the time she got past the opening credits. Thirty minutes later she would finish and I would be nodding my head. I loved my sister. I just didn't have the heart to tell her. Over the years she learned to tell the *Readers Digest* condensed version. Today she is an executive with Johnson & Johnson.

3) **Speak too slowly.**

People have very short attention spans. Most companies pitch their products in thirty-second commercials on television. The newest wave of men's magazines include the best sellers *Stuff* and *Maxim*. These publications feature "articles" as short as a paragraph. Our attention spans are so short that *USA Today* seems to be filled with articles that are far too detailed for a lot of people. The message needs to be delivered quickly and concisely in print and in everyday conversation.

One of the greatest problems people have when telling a story is speaking far too slowly. Think of the people who are enjoyable to listen to. Comedians. Robin Williams: Speaks quickly. Dennis Miller: Speaks quickly. Bill Cosby: Speaks moderately. George Wallace: Speaks quickly. Billy Crystal: Moderate to fast paced. Jerry Seinfeld: Moderate to fast paced.

There aren't a lot of people who can make you laugh who also speak slowly when they are telling a story. Yes, there is an exception to every rule, but here is the rule: Speak a little more quickly and you have a better chance of having your story heard and enjoyed.

4) Speak in a garbled way so that people can't understand you.

Many people look away when they are communicating with you. They think you have a universal translator that translates all languages including garbled English. Remember that millions of people are hard of hearing and they have little chance of hearing the average woman (who speak at frequencies much higher than men) speak at all.

When you speak, look at the person you are talking to. Speak clearly. Speak loudly enough so everyone can hear you. All of this may seem obvious, but having observed thousands of people communicate, I promise you that this one mistake causes big problems in relationships . . . problems that could easily be avoided.

5) Exaggerate when telling your story.

". . . and there were millions of people watching the parade . . ."

(There were 850 according to newspaper accounts.)

". . . I never even looked at her . . ."

(Never looked?!)

". . . before he started the diet he weighed 300 pounds . . ."

(Okay, it was really 240.)

A story worth telling is worth telling accurately. Tell it with enthusiasm, zeal, and intensity. Tell it accurately. Later in the chapter I'll show you how to tell a story that holds interest, builds your credibility, and engages your listener. For now, it's vital that all of your communication be true without being critical or unnecessarily unkind. Exaggeration is an invitation for people to not listen or care.

6) Ignore feedback during your storytelling.

". . . and then she comes in the door and she has this skirt on that is so ridiculously short. I mean, who is she kidding? She's not a teenager anymore."

(Friend nods politely while fighting back a yawn, eyes begin to glaze over.)

" . . . do people have no sense of decency anymore? I just wonder what makes some people tick. Don't people pay attention to what they are wearing and see how it makes everybody feel?"

(Friend shrugs and nods with feigned frustration.)

The woman telling the story about the short-skirted office friend could have spared her listener the despair of this antiquated story had she only seen the feigned frustration, the shrug, the yawn . . . but it was not something the storyteller was looking for. It should have been. It's critical to always pay attention to how people are receiving the stories you tell.

You must pay close attention to your listeners' body language while you are telling your story. Is their body language telling you they are interested or impatient for the end? Are their lips moving, ready to jump in on your story, or are they listening with awe. Later in the book we will discuss body language in depth. Not learning to understand the body language of other people is one of the mistakes we make in communication.

7) Respond to other people's stories with a story of your own.

". . . and I went to Cancun and you should have seen the beaches. They were beautiful. The Princess Hotel was absolutely breathtak . . ."

"You stayed at the Princess? It's really not bad you know. On our third trip to Cancun we stayed at the Princess, in the Oceanview Suite. They reserved it for us because John helped with the design of the building in '98. I didn't really like the Princess that much. It was a wannabee hotel. But since then we've stayed at the new Sheraton. It just has everything and they take care of you like you are royalty there. I think if we go back and don't go to Tahiti on our next trip, we're going to stay there again."

"Cancun sure is nice."

(The energy has been discharged from her being and the desire to communicate further with her friend went with her energy.)

This is one of the really sad things we do in communicating with others. Instead of teasing out the rest of the story from our friend, we immediately jump in with a story of our own. Research shows that people feel better when you pursue their story to its completion and then disclose (share) something of your own.

8) Poke holes in other people's special stories.

They are telling you about their adventure in the audit at the Internal Revenue Service office.

"I was so nervous, I'm driving to the IRS office and I'm sitting there thinking, oh man, I have to remember to NOT talk. Shut up. Be quiet. Don't say anything."

"What did you do to get audited?"

"Huh? I filed Schedule C and that means . . ."

"Did you report all of your income?"

"I think so."

"You THINK so? What are you, nuts? You have to report all of your income."

"Of course you have to report all of your income. Anyway, I'm on the way to the IRS office and . . ."

"Did you overstate your deductions?"

"Of course not. I . . ."

"If you overstate your deductions they will bust your . . ."

"I KNOW that, and I didn't. Let's just drop the whole thing."

"Okay. I was just trying to help."

And so it goes. Our storyteller was preparing to tell the story of her big victory over the IRS auditor and our storyteller's friend poked big holes in the story—so big that it took all the fun and excitement out of sharing the story.

The appropriate response would have been to listen with fascination and a sense of curiosity, saving all questions and comments for much, much later.

9) Overtly brag about yourself too much.

"I don't want to brag, but the place would have gone under without me. I was there every day at dawn and stayed 'til the sun went down. I built the company and once they had 100 employees there was no appreciation at all. They down-sized me. It was unbelievable. I literally designed almost every major piece that we produced and when it came time for them to decide who to let go, it was me. I couldn't believe it. They never would have gone public without me. They never would have met their payroll without me. I just can't believe they didn't see what I was worth to them."

True or not, bragging never pays. There are so many effective ways to bolster your reputation and communication credentials when talking to people that you never need to overstate your contribution to a relationship, a project, a business, a deal, or anything. Later you'll learn how to tell a great story where you were a hero without bragging at all!

10) Not telling your stories with intention.

Before you begin speaking, override the compulsion to blurt out your story.

Think:

What is the intention of your story?
Why are you going to tell this story?
Will anyone who listens to this story be hurt by what you say?

You might think that it's not that important to communicate exactly what you mean, but remember December 2002? Quite often someone tells a story and they haven't thought about who they are telling the story to or how it might easily be misinterpreted to mean something else.

Sen. Trent Lott, a Mississippi Republican, got himself stuck in a public relations nightmare in December 2002 and paid a severe price. Destined to regain his position as the Senate Majority Leader in January of 2003, he made a critical mistake that everyone should be attentive to and learn from.

Speaking at a party honoring Sen. Strom Thurmond on his 100th birthday, Lott opened Pandora's box and never knew what his words of appreciation for the elderly senator would do. The drama of misunderstood words caused even the President of the United States to distance himself from Lott.

Speaking for the President, White House Press Secretary Ari Fleischer said after one speech that Bush was not calling for Lott to step aside as leader or as senator.

"The President does not think that Senator Lott needs to resign," Fleischer said.

The problem? Thurmond, the South Carolina Republican who ran as a third-party candidate for president in 1948 as a segregationist, had changed his views over the ensuing fifty years of public service. But the comments by Lott made it appear that Lott was still in favor of them. In 1948 most blacks in many southern U.S. states, including Mississippi, were not allowed to vote.

Lott actually didn't say anything that was racist, but the interpretation by his adversaries was easy to spin into the public mind. Shortly after the speech, Lott called Bush, and his office issued a statement saying the President was right.

"Senator Lott agrees with President Bush that his words were wrong and he is sorry," said Lott spokesman Ron Bonjean. "He repudiates segregation because it is immoral."

Lott expressed similar sentiments in his call to Bush, Fleischer said.

So just what did Lott say at the Thurmond celebration?

". . . . we're proud of it. And if the rest of the country had followed our lead, we wouldn't have had all these problems over the years."

Later, he would have to clarify what he meant, but it was too late. He hadn't thought through how his words might effect the minds of his greatest adversaries.

"I'm sorry for my words," said Lott, who had said he would not step aside as Senate Republican leader. Speaking to WABC Radio in New York and then on BET Television days later, Lott said he had wanted to honor "Thurmond the man," but not back segregationist policies.

The Congressional Black Caucus called for a formal censure of Lott, saying anything less would be seen as approval of his remarks by Bush, Congress, and the

Republican Party. In Mississippi, civil rights officials said his apology was insufficient, and accused him of having enduring ties to groups that are believed to have racist views. Several major U.S. newspapers published editorials demanding Republicans reject Lott as their Senate leader.

A few misunderstood words cost Lott his reputation and drove many of those closest to him to leave his side.

Lesson: *When telling your stories, think about how they will be received by your listeners . . . and the people your listeners will talk to. You aren't likely to ever be under media scrutiny like a political leader, but the point is clear. Think before speaking.*

In a conversation with friends, business colleagues, and the like you will often hear them say something that frustrates you. You will hear things that you don't understand. Because you really want to know what the person means and feels, you must learn to tease out the intention.

Did they mean what you thought they just said?
Did they mean what you heard?

In Lott's case, a friend might say to the Senator, "So are you saying you liked the way Thurmond thought about segregation in 1948."

He might reply, "Of course not. What a stupid thought. I meant that I really admire Thurmond."

It is that simple . . . and difficult. When you don't

understand their story, seek to understand before criticizing the person!

WHO ARE YOU?

The most important element of a story is that it tells who you are. Without knowing this, the listener is not interested in giving you the time of day.

To tell a story that captivates others it is necessary to first share "who you are." People need to know why they should listen to you. I once heard Zig Ziglar say, "People don't care what you know until they know that you care." I've always believed that and tried to live that.

Sharing "who you are" means detailing what actions others see in you and stating things in their terms. In other words, you don't say, "I knew I was great because the audience applauded." You say, "And when the audience applauded, I felt so good inside!"

Here are a couple of more examples:
"I'm a generous person."
Vs.
"All I had was a $1 bill in my pocket, but I knew that it might buy someone a sandwich at the Salvation Army so I threw it in the bucket."

"I'm a nice person."
"I had no idea if the lady was going to be mad at me or not for helping her across the street, but I took my chances and took her arm."

"I show my love every time I get a chance."
"When I was on the phone with my son, he said,

'Dad, you're the greatest Dad in the world.' I said, 'I love you bigger than the planet Jupiter.'"

One way of communicating is quickly labeled as bragging. The other way allows you to tell your story about specific incidents that happened, and the difference can be that of captivation and fascination or boredom.

MAKE IT KNOWN THAT YOU ARE HUMAN

When you tell a story, you must be certain that you highlight your weaknesses. There are many kinds of weaknesses. Most can be highlighted in a self-deprecating or fun way and your listener will like you all the more if you point them out.

"I've never been the smartest guy on the street . . ."

"Okay, so my body runs like an old Pinto, but I still get around . . ."

"I was never good looking but my premature balding took the pressure off everyone staring at my face . . ."

Poke fun at yourself and you take away the desire for others to do it for you. It's quite charming to reveal a few of your inner thoughts (so long as they are going to be well tolerated by your audience).

YOUR STORY SHOULD INSPIRE

Tell someone how great you are and they will dismiss you. Tell your story as a human who was driven to accomplish something in spite of your frailties and you will find yourself having an audience chomping at the bit to hear more from you.

Everyone has a story tell. In fact, we all have a bag

full of stories to share. I am going to show you how to identify the ways you can overcome the common mistakes people make when storytelling. Next, I want to share with you three of my stories woven together, and I want you to learn some things about me.

Here are my goals (my intention) with telling the next three stories:

1) I want you to see my devotion and dedication to my family.
2) I want you to see that I have struggled with my self worth.
3) I want you to know I have a sense of humor.
4) I want you to know that I survived and became successful despite personal weaknesses in my ability to communicate well.
5) I don't want to have to say any of these things overtly because I don't want to turn you off with bragging or feeling sorry for me.

Winter 1972

I (KH) started my own "business" when I was 10 years old. I had to. I was the oldest of five children and we had no money. My stepfather was going to die in less than eighteen months and Mom's time was divided between her job and taking care of Dad, who was confined to a hospital bed in our home. It was a heck of a way to live. We lived in a "lower-middle-class" suburb of Chicago. If I wanted to have money for anything (and I did), I would have to sell something.

I sold my services in the wintertime as the kid on the street who would shovel your driveway. $1 per hour.

The Chicago winds would blow out of the north and off the lake with a bitter coldness that I'll never forget. Sometimes I'd take the $3 I would earn and give it to Mom. Sometimes I'd keep the money and buy Pepsi and Reese's. In the summer, I would sell my services cutting people's lawns or pulling weeds. (I hated pulling weeds.)

Realizing that there was no hope for me in the lawn and garden services, I knew at age 10 I would have to do something where I could utilize my time in a far more efficient manner. I saw an ad in a Sunday newspaper for Cheerful House Greeting Cards. I read that I could earn from fifty cents to two dollars for each box of cards sold.

I immediately sent the company my $10 for a sample kit. ($10 was a lot of money in those days.) In return, Cheerful House sent me five boxes of Christmas cards. Some quick math calculations revealed that if I just sold the five boxes I'd make $1 per box sold! The sales literature said that there would be only four "selling seasons" per year, so whatever money was going to be earned would have to last a LONG time.

I got home from school the next day, and as soon as my paper route was done I was ready to go make some real money! I knocked on my neighbor's door. It was Mrs. Gossard. I showed her my cards and she bought a box. My first dollar was earned! Then I went to Mrs. Singer. (She couldn't buy a box.) Mrs. Hendricks bought two boxes, Mrs. Serdar bought a box. Mrs. Makela bought a box. Lots of other people didn't.

I was gone until 8 p.m. and had knocked on thirty doors and sold about eighteen boxes of cards. I looked at my watch as the sun was setting. I knew I had to go home and help put the kids to bed. I had checks totaling about $60, of which my math whiz brain figured, $20 was mine.

Mom was so excited when she saw the order sheet. I told her that I'd give her all the money I earned. She said, "No. You earned it, you are going to keep it." Wow! The next day I left the neighborhood to start selling in a neighborhood I never went to. I was out from the time my paper route was done until sunset. I sold only four boxes of cards. Some of the people's houses were scary looking and, being a skinny little kid, I decided that I wouldn't go back there again!

Nevertheless, I made about $4. I showed it to Mom when I got home, and she told me that it was mine to keep.

The problem was that I knocked on about fifty doors to earn that $4. I couldn't believe that more people didn't buy my Christmas cards. They obviously weren't as smart as the people in my neighborhood. The next day was Saturday and I remember getting up, delivering the Saturday morning *Waukegan New-Sun* (they had to be delivered by 7 a.m.!), cutting the lawn, and then at noon off I went on my bicycle. I went into neighborhoods I had never been to and knocked on over 100 doors that day. I didn't stop to eat lunch or dinner. I sold six boxes of cards.

I got home to find that there was no Hamburger Helper left. (I was eternally grateful.) I told Mom that I didn't have a very good day. I made $6 but I was driving across highways and I was kind of scared of the neighborhoods I was going into. She suggested I stick with the neighborhoods where people knew me and where I wouldn't be crossing the highways anymore. (She would later tell me she was scared to death that her son was going into some of the neighborhoods!)

We totaled the order sheet. I had sold twenty-eight boxes of cards. My total earnings would be about $30. I would get paid after I delivered all of the cards to my clients. I couldn't wait!

I learned a lot that week.

I learned that selling cards was a lot better than cutting the lawn, pulling weeds, shoveling the snow, or delivering the newspaper.

I learned I could only work four weeks per year selling cards. Selling cards was going to make me $100 per year next year but I'd need to think of something else to sell if I was going to make more money.

More importantly, after delivering the cards to the people a few weeks earlier, I realized how much fun it was to see people smile and say, "Thanks, Kevin." "They're beautiful." "You got those to me faster than I expected."

Most importantly, I made $30 for about twenty hours of work that was not physically killing my scrawny 10-year-old body!

I sold greeting cards for the next four years as a source of income. I sold flower seeds and vegetable seeds. (I also continued to sell my body shoveling snow, pulling weeds, cutting lawns, and doing anything else I could.) The most fun was selling cards, though. The women were (for the most part) fun to talk with, the work was all sitting down in their living room, and some of them even gave me cookies and milk those few days per year when I was selling. I was actually having fun working at something.

The ad from Cheerful House Greeting Cards changed my life. Not because it made me rich. It didn't. It gave me hope that I could escape living in poverty. The Boy Scouts wouldn't need to bring me clothes and turkey dinners on Thanksgiving any more. (The Boy Scouts delivered clothing and food to our home on Thanksgiving on a couple of occasions. I remember appreciating the clothes and food . . . and hating being needy.) I knew that what I was going to do when I was older would be selling.

I was right.

I discovered as a 10-year-old that the ability to think quickly and talk with people could give me a chance to escape being poor, and maybe—just maybe—be rich. Selling was hard work in some ways, but it was fun. It certainly beat "physical work."

Selling would give me security, freedom, inde-pendence, and the ability to be productive . . . to be valuable to other people. It was something I could do well.

Fast forward to 1998.

Autumn 1998

I had been earning a six-figure income for a few years. I've owned my own business, consulted, or sold for other people since 1987. The idea of receiving an hourly wage and punching a time clock is almost a pho-bia. Business is good. I have several books in print, including one, *The Psychology of Persuasion,* that is doing pretty darned well in the bookstores. But . . .

I stalled. I stagnated. I was earning $1,000-$2,000 per speech. Nothing wrong with that, but I've been there and done that. No one was offering me more than that. I am baffled. People compare my speaking style to that of Anthony Robbins and my physical and offstage presence to Kelsey Grammar, David Letterman, and Drew Carey. Now, what more could a guy want? That's enough talent to feed off of for FOUR lifetimes.

Enter Dottie Walters, the author of *Speak and Grow Rich.* (Dottie owns the world's most prestigious speakers bureau and publishes *Sharing Ideas* magazine for national speakers.)

I see her "Speak and Grow Rich" course listed next to mine in the Open U catalog. I have no time to take a full day off and learn what I already know, regardless of whom it is with. But for years I have been wanting to meet Dottie. She would now be about 70, or maybe older, and it was her book *Speak and Grow Rich* that helped me focus my world on teaching and speaking in public for a significant portion of my current livelihood.

I decided to take the Saturday off and go see Dottie. If nothing else, I would thank her for being inspirational in my life!

I attended her class with about twenty other students. I enjoyed watching the woman speak for five hours. She was able to keep the group enthralled with stories she had no doubt told for decades. Her approach was simple and somewhat grandmotherly. She was kind and direct. I was in love. (Not to mention that watching her do back-of-the-room sales was inspiring!)

I didn't get what I came for, though. I hadn't really learned anything new. But I was in love. I approached her after everyone had left the class and her grandson had finished packing the few books and videos that hadn't been snatched up by the audience.

"Dottie, I'm Kevin Hogan. I want you to know you have been an inspiration in my career."

"Thank you, Kevin." She looked up into my eyes. She was tired. I've been here before. The last person wants to keep you forever. You (I) have been on stage for six hours and you want to find the bed in the hotel and fall flat on your face and have them wake you in fifteen hours for breakfast.

"Dottie, I want you to have this." (I hand her my book *The Psychology of Persuasion.*)

"Thank you, dear."

Okay, Kevin, her brain is fading. Either ask or get the hell out of here. She has a date with a hotel pillow and you are being as charming as a bottle of mental Drano.

"Dottie, I have one question for you. I have been doing about $1,500 per speech for the last couple of years. It doesn't change. They don't offer more than $2,000. What do you suggest? You tell me, I'll do it. Anything. What is going to take me to the next ($5,000+) level?"

"Have you asked, Kevin?"

"Pardon me?"

"Have you asked for $5,000?"

"Well, not really. I mean . . . no . . . you know, I haven't."

She put her hand on my arm and patted me like I was a little child.

"Well honey, just ask." She looked at my book and smiled. "Just ask."

"Thanks, Dottie, I will."

As I walked out of the door on that brisk Minneapolis afternoon, I wondered just how stupid I must have looked. Successful author towers over sweet woman asking the dumbest question on the face of the earth. Thank God no one would ever know about this moment.

Fast forward: one month.

Early Winter 1998

I have a sore throat and a terrible cold. My nose is stuffier than it ever has been. I feel terrible. CNBC is on in the background. The market is not doing well and I'm not making money today.

(Ring)

"Who could that be?" I talk to CNBC when no one else is around.

"Kevin Hogan, can I help you?" (It didn't sound like that. Maybe they bought it on the other end.)

"Is this Dr. Hogan?"

"Yes it is." (Dr. Hogan has actually left the building for dead. This is his associate who has not yet succumbed to the flu.)

"Oh, you sound terrible. This is Richard Marks (not his real name) with the Sales Association (not their real name either)."

"How can I help you?"

"Well, we were at your website and are looking for a speaker for our winter meeting in Minneapolis. What are you charging nowadays?"

Here it is, Kevin. You spent the last month finishing Talk Your Way to the Top. *It's over. The book is at Pelican. What are you going to tell this guy? Your voice sounds like hell. You've just yelled at CNBC. You . . . just ask, honey. Just ask . . . .*

"*$5,000 is my fee, but I'd sure like to know more about your group and what you are looking for.*"

Richard tells me about his group, tells me they want me to talk about "body language," and asks if I will settle on $4,000, which is what his budget is approved for. What's the difference between 4K and 5K anyway? You're working for ONE HOUR, Kevin? You moron. It's an hour drive and you are working for an hour. Just ask honey . . . just ask.

"No, my fee is $5,000, and I think I can give you exactly what you are looking for. An hour of massive entertainment combined with an hour of data, all happening simultaneously."

"I'll have to check for approval on $5,000. I'll call you back. Thanks, Kevin, we'll talk soon."

I thought to myself, "You stupid moron." (CNBC was running a commercial with Ringo Starr in it. I could use a little help from my friends, Ringo . . .) *"What the heck are you thinking? Guaranteed $4,000. Been paid that once for a full day, never for an hour, and you say, $5,000. Idiot. Idiot. Idiot."*

Sue Herrera talks with Ron Insana about how the market is taking a hit today, and I'm feeling like a bigger idiot by the micro-second. The phone doesn't ring for the rest of the day.

Fast forward: next day.

(Ring)

"Kevin Hogan."

"That really you?"

"Who's this?"

"Richard Marks."

"Hi, Richard, good to hear your voice." *(I'll take the $4,000. Just offer it again, now, and I'm yours.)*

"Kevin we got the $5,000 approved and would like you to . . . . blah blah blah blah . . ." *(Get out of here. DOTTIE, I LOVE YOU. Just ask, honey . . . . I never doubted you, Dottie, I swear to . . . just ask . . . and I wrote* THE PSYCHOLOGY OF PERSUASION. *I mean, how long does it take to realize that you are unable to follow your own advice? Just ask, honey. . . . DOTTIE, YOU ARE THE GREATEST.)*

"How does that sound, Kevin?"

"Yes, absolutely, let's run through the details again. My head is foggy from this flu."

Deal closed. Check received in six business days. That was the last time I doubted that still, small sweet voice in my head. Dottie is with me always . . .

Have you ever suffered from low self-esteem? We all do. I tell you this story because every time I think of it I remember that I'm worth an enormous amount to people, to society, to myself. I also think of my childhood because it reminds me that no matter how tough things get, they aren't going to be that bad ever again.

Lesson 1. Through the stories in this chapter I was able to teach you about my dedication to my family when I was a child. You learned that I cared about my family. You learned that I wanted to take care of them.

Lesson 2. Through the stories in this chapter you learned my exact process of finally asking to be paid what I am worth. You saw my struggle with my own self-esteem and discovered that you are a lot like me. If I can do it you can do it. That message was critical to get through from my conscious mind to your unconscious mind.

Lesson 3. You now know that I have been successful in the field of influence and are therefore more likely to accept what I tell you as factual; therefore you are more likely to act upon those messages.

Lesson 4. I have disclosed personal weaknesses to you so you know that I am not a superman . . . nor do I think I am. If you want people to like you and respect you, you must let them know that you are not arrogant. You are just like they are.

Chapter Three

The Forgotten Art of Listening

One of the greatest gifts ever bestowed on mankind by God, Goddess, Spirit, Wakan Tanka, Allah, Buddha, Fred, Ethel—whatever name you choose to call your higher belief—is the gift of **hearing.** We hear things around us every day and call this sound. Sound (auditory stimulus), whether by music, Mother Nature, everyday speech, or the words of a loved one, is a wonderful thing. But that is not what this chapter is about at all.

Consider for just a moment the magic of **listening.** I want to talk with you about the way we sometimes forget to listen and begin to only *hear* people instead. Or even worse yet, we begin to *"already always know"* what the other person is saying and tune them out, making up our own version of what they are trying to tell us.

Sometimes we get so busy that we don't even listen to the words that the people we work with, interact with, or even say we love are really saying. I want to discuss with you the forgotten little things, which we tend to think as not important at all, such as not listening to the words of those we *don't* love. But maybe we should.

True listening is a magnetic and strangely elusive force sometimes, a creature that begs to be acknowledged. Just for a moment, think about the people in your past that you have been attracted to or who have made an important impact on you. You know, the people in your life that have made a difference and helped develop who you are right now. Chances are these were the same people who **didn't** share the vast knowledge of life they had acquired with you. The ones who perhaps **weren't** gracious enough to bestow upon you the gift of their worldly advice.

People who found it unnecessary to entertain you with tall tales of their life experiences, offering you insights (i.e., advice) into *your* personality that they deemed unworthy so that you could be more like them . . . in other words: perfect. Instead, these people gave you one small gift, maybe one that seemed insignificant at the time, yet it was an enormously precious gift. They gave you their time and their ability to listen without judgment.

We have all known people who when we begin to talk to them seem distracted, or too eager to share *their* version of *your* story. You know the ones I mean: the ones who hear without listening, just waiting for the right moment to pounce in and tell your story in "other words." These are the people in our lives who *"already always know"* what you are about to say. They have their own filters of what you are saying and anticipate everything that is *about* to come out of your mouth, whether they have guessed right or wrong.

The problem here is most of the time they ARE wrong, and it's frustrating to the person *telling* the story or sharing their emotions to have to keep repeating themselves in the midst of constant interruptions, trying to regain control of the conversation.

Often, as this happens, the narrator quits in frustration and clams up, retreating inward, and the mood of the interaction between the two parties is endangered.

"Hey, you look great! Nice tan! Have you been on vacation?"

"Yes, Jeanie and I spent three weeks in Hawaii."

"Fantastic. I was there once. What did you two end up doing?"

"Well, the first day we spent on the beach relaxing, and then we went . . ."

"Oh, then you probably spent the rest of the day at the volcanoes, right?"

"No, we went . . ."

"Okay, then you must have gone snorkeling. I bet the fish were fantastic!"

"No, we just rested the first day because of the plane trip. But then that night we . . ."

"Then you guys MUST have gone to the nightly luau, right? I bet it was a blast; all that good food and entertainment."

"NO, WE didn't . . ."

"Then what DID you two end up doing there?"

"Never mind, wasn't important. We just had a good time and came home."

Let the person speaking tell his/her version of the story.

The friends that really listen to us are the ones we move toward, the ones we want to spend time with, sitting in their "presence," feeling their warmth. They make us feel good, comfortable, and secure. We can tell them our thoughts, dreams, and hopes and share our tears and shed the cloak of our fears, all without fear of criticism, judgment, or competition.

The reason: When someone listens to us, it helps to create **US,** makes **US** unfold and expand ourselves. Our ideas have a place to be planted, germinate, grow within us and come to life. When someone pays attention, really *listening* to us instead of just *hearing* us, listening without being judgmental, it allows and encourages us to share our innermost thoughts, feelings that we normally would be afraid to speak because we are afraid of our words being misinterpreted or ridiculed.

Help someone create himself by listening to him.

Have you ever noticed that if a person laughs at your jokes, you want to become funnier, enjoying the acceptance and begin striving for more attention? And if they DON'T laugh, all time seems to stop, every millisecond seems like a week, your face begins to feel flushed, and suddenly it gets very hot in the room. Every little joke, every tiny speck of humor inside you weakens and dies as you begin to question your very right to breathe the earth's air? Okay, so that's a bit dramatic, but here are a few scenarios of what could be going on here:

- ✔ Maybe you simply picked the wrong joke; not all humor is funny to all people all the time.

- ✔ Maybe you just can't TELL a joke. Sadly, most of us don't have that talent and we *still* keep trying in vain to be funny, or worse yet, we believe we really are funny and others just don't have a sense of humor.

✔ Maybe others don't understand the joke. (*Please* don't explain it to us; if we don't get it the first time, we never will. We just give that courtesy laugh because we feel sorry for you for telling us lame jokes.)

✔ Maybe they have already heard the joke.

✔ And finally, maybe, just maybe, they have their own internal version of what is being said. They have *heard* you instead of *listened* to you.

---

*Know your audience, use discrimination,
and don't tell jokes.*

When you "listen" to another's words, then turn those words around to "hear" them in a different context, you aren't "listening." You are "interpreting" what they are saying and shutting out what they really mean. You are putting your own meaning on their thoughts. We all are guilty of this at times. Humans are just built to be "meaning-making machines" and we put our private stamp on everything that happens around us to make it understandable to us.

But there are many benefits to being a good listener. It makes people happy to be listened to. Listening is the golden key; it unlocks the secret treasure box of having a good time in society because everyone around you suddenly becomes lively and interesting. It's the secret of comforting people, of doing them good, of truly learning what and how your friends, family, in fact everyone around you, views the world.

> *A good listener is often perceived as a brilliant conversationalist.*

Ask yourself: who do you go to for advice? Probably not to the hard, critical, practical people who tend to tell you exactly what to do, but to the listeners—the kindest, non-censoring, non-judgmental people you know. It is because we feel at liberty to share our heart-felt outpouring of emotions, trials/tribulations, and problems with them. It is because of their non-judgment that we become aware of what to do about it ourselves.

We can all be our own best advisors if we have someone who is willing to give us a neutral sounding board to express our views and make our own decisions about what to do with them.

I (RS) once had a small 6-year-old child as a client in my therapy office who taught me more than any teacher I've ever studied with. I was listening to him tell me about how some of the older kids were picking on him in school. He had told his parents, his teachers, even the principal; but no one had believed his story. They kept insisting he was being "too sensitive" and blowing things out of proportion. He couldn't understand why someone didn't believe his story.

Then, in his very young but wise way, he gave me some very valuable advice about listening. He said,

"God gave us two ears and one mouth so that we could listen twice as much as we talk."

Use your two ears and listen twice as much as you speak.

"Lights down, champagne poured, candles lit; cue the orchestra."

Remember when you first fell in love with that special person? Or had that best date ever with the man or woman of your dreams? You shared your dreams, hopes, and plans with each other. You might have listened intently to every word the other said, gazing into one another's eyes, hanging on every thought. You made him/her feel like they were the only one that mattered in the entire world, and they made you feel that way too. That night seemed to last forever.

Nice, wasn't it? You didn't just *hear* each other; you *listened* to each other.

Then somewhere in the relationship, you might have quit listening. You began to know each other so well that you finished each other's sentences and thoughts. You began to *hear* **instead of** *listen* to one another. You began to predict your partner's thoughts and ideas and expected him/her to read your mind as well. You probably became frustrated when your "predictions" didn't match their thoughts (because, after all, YOUR version was right).

You might have become even more frustrated when they couldn't read your mind and you expected them to "know" what you meant even though you never said it out loud. Then you might have added two and two together, come up with three, and figured that the magic of the relationship was lost. Nope, you simply quit listening.

In this wide, wide world, there are truly brilliant people who can speak for hours, waxing eloquently on poetry, literary works, and art and who are truly fascinating orators. They can talk, give lectures and speeches, captivating us by expressing their heartfelt emotions. They can bring a tear to our eyes and entertain us for hours with their witty conversation.

Yet some of these same people can also bore us to tears and leave us feeling exhausted, as if we have just run a 26-mile marathon. Why? Because they never listen. It's all about them.

But why does this failure to listen exhaust us?

People who don't give us a chance, an opportunity to share and express ourselves, to be **US,** put out our spark, our flame. It is this spark, our spirit, this fire, this waterfall within us all that drives us and makes us whole. This constant, ever-changing flow of energy is what makes us, **US.**

In our fast-paced, fast-food, go-go-go, hurry-up, we're-going-to-be-late world, we have a tendency to get over-tired, strained, over-stressed, and over-stimulated. We have no solitude into which we can retreat. We get too busy, talk to too many people during the course of our day, overextend ourselves so that our waterfall of energy gets dirty and dim, covered with the slime, mud, sticks, stones, and garbage of life.

The result is that we stop living from the inside, from that waterfall of energy within us, and start living life from the outside, the external. We stop *listening* and begin *hearing*. We plod along, day to day, going through the motions of life without truly living.

Many times when we are not given a chance to talk, when we cannot express our innermost thoughts and desires, that waterfall begins to "dry up" inside. We don't allow new ideas and thoughts to spring up, we suppress unexpected things within ourselves, like laughter, silliness, and wisdom.

Maybe that is why when someone has truly listened to you, really been INSIDE you, listened with fascinated, rapt attention, made YOU feel like you were the most important person on earth to them, you feel better, lighter, more at peace with everything around you.

Beginning tomorrow, instead of thinking *"I must share myself with everyone I meet today. I'll be gregarious, outgoing, sociable, and funny. I'll be someone people will listen to and admire for my wit, my talent, and charm,"* why not allow yourself to truly **listen.** Not just **hear** someone speak, but focus on **listening** to them, be in their shoes when they talk, see the world through their eyes, experience life from their point of view instead of being compelled to express your own.

Listen without judgment or advice. Allow the person talking to show his/her soul to you. Treat them like they are the most important person on earth. Now is their time to shine in the light, to take center stage and to be the star attraction.

They may be a little taken back and unsure at first that it is possible to trust you not to interrupt, to not try and show them up or judge them, because very few people in their lives have ever taken the time to listen.

After all, listening **IS** a forgotten, fine art. So become a great artist. Grab your brush and start practicing the art of listening instead of simply hearing. Keep practicing, and when you think you have it down to a science, go practice some more.

Now go paint your masterpiece.

Chapter Four

Arguing with the Intent to Harm

THE ARGUMENTATIVE COMMUNICATOR

Do you enjoy playing the devil's advocate? Are you constantly offering your opposing opinion when it is not asked for? Do you find yourself saying the word "but" often in your conversation with others? You may be an argumentative talker.

There is an effective way to take an opposing view, but it may destroy rapport. There is a way to give your opinion, but it may be received as unwanted advice. When you continue to oppose the comments of your listener, you run the risk of making him/her feel wrong, stupid, or uninformed.

Men and women seem to view communication differences in different ways. I often notice that men will say, "we had a debate" or "an intense conversation" and women will indicate that they had "a fight" or an "argument."

The argumentative communicator, whether a man or a woman, should be aware that their communication efforts may immediately be perceived as a "fight" (the worst of the four above labels) regardless of the intent of the communicator.

I have a confession to make. I was in debate in high
school and, like Jack Welch (former CEO of General
Electric), I find a good debate stimulating and enlight-
ening. Debate generally can be described as a struc-
tured discussion where individuals cite evidence about
an issue in an attempt to persuade another person.
Debate is an intellectual process where it is okay and
preferable to be "right." While I do enjoy debating very
much, I do not enjoy arguing, which is emotionally
based.

Arguing is where two or more people disagree about
some subject. They raise their voices and make the discussion personal by predicting the other person's
intentions and then assigning blame or labeling people
as "stupid" or something equally as divisive.

What's the difference then between debate and an
argument?

In debate, we cite evidence with the intent to validate
our point of view. Debate is all about intellectual conflict where people try to convince each other who is
right and who has the best evidence. In arguments, we
cite evidence, make claims about the negative intention of the other person's behavior, and become very
emotional to the point where apologies will be in order
after the communication is finished because one or
both parties will have their feelings hurt.

In an argument, the individual feels attacked. When
the attack is perceived as hostile, with *intention to harm,*
I call this a "fight."

Perceptions are tricky things. One person may be
simply debating or discussing a subject intellectually
with no intent to harm. The other person may perceive

such communication as intending to harm them and they feel as if they are in a fight with a need to defend themselves instead of their point of view! Sometimes it takes quite a long time for the person who is debating to come to the discovery and conclusion that the other person is upset and fighting.

There are no easy and clearly defined answers to rapidly determine whether someone thinks you are arguing, fighting, debating, or discussing. Therefore it is vital to ask if it's "okay to have this conversation," or at least smile. It's also important to keep sarcasm out of discussions and debates if it isn't obvious to the other person that you are having fun *with* him instead of poking fun *at* him.

The argumentative communicator needs to be right. He wants to defeat his opponent, as if the dining room or boardroom is a courtroom where only one person can "win." In interpersonal communications or in business, it's critical to remember that it's very easy for no one to win. This doesn't mean to stop disagreeing or intellectually pursuing what is good and right. It is very important to make sure those we have discussions with do not feel attacked.

Therefore it's important to make your intention known to your partner and to tease out the intention in his/her communication if you feel attacked.

Conflict is central to change and progress in life, religion, science, and relationships.

There is an additional problem. You and I both know that we often take possession of our ideas as if they were our identity. People protect their ideas and beliefs like drug addicts do their drugs. If one's ideas and verbalized thoughts are always experienced at the level of one's identity, then all debate will become perceived as fighting or arguing.

Therefore when this pattern of communication erupts, it's important to separate the idea from the person. This doesn't stop discussion and debates from becoming arguments and fights but it does add clarity to the conversation.

Always discuss the issue and leave the person alone if possible!

If you are discussing something with someone and he perceives you as argumentative, I suggest you ask the person, "How can I present counter examples and other points of view to you so that you are not offended and your feelings are not hurt?" I have thought of this wonderful question many times when it was simply too late to ask.

If you experience numerous people saying things like, "you just love to argue, don't you?" or "why do you always argue with me?" or "I don't want to fight with you," then regardless of whether you are fighting or not you need to reconsider your approach to communication so you are perceived as less abrasive.

Many times people who are intellectuals (whether they are "intellectual snobs" or not!) are considered argumentative simply because they have such a broad or deep knowledge about something that they are constantly the individual with superior knowledge about a subject. This can lead others to feeling inferior.

In these situations, it can be useful for the person perceived as superior, and therefore the one who often puts others "on edge" or "on the defensive," to reduce the number of verbalizations in a communication and "tighten up his communication." Make long speeches shorter. Ask more questions and have fewer total words spoken in dialogue.

Remember: Where one person seems to know everything, the other person is not necessary . . . or at least that's how the other can feel.

Most brilliant people got that way because they were incredibly inquisitive. This too can become a problem! Asking questions of others is a great way to learn about how others feel, think, and believe, but believe it or not there are lines that can be crossed here as well!

Many people process their "thoughts" through their "feelings." You can ask someone what he is thinking, and he may say, "I don't know," "nothing," "not much," "nothing important," and so on. Such people aren't planning major life events in their mind. They are simply in the moment . . . in their feelings. And because they process information differently from verbalizing thinkers, they often feel inadequate in a relationship or are pegged as poor communicators. In fact, they may not be good communicators, but they can improve their communication skills if others don't put an enormous amount of pressure on them.

If you are a person who takes time to process external information and you don't communicate well about information you have just received, a good strategy to appear more competent is to say things such as: "I need to consider what you've said, to ponder it." "Let

me think about what you've said. I'd like to talk with
you tomorrow about it, when I've taken the time it
deserves." "My initial reaction is positive and I'd like to
take some more time to consider it."

What this does is allow the two parties to know that
there is no problem with what was communicated by
the verbalizing party and that they are indeed considering the information, not ignoring it as verbalizers
often feel others are doing "to them."

"Nonverbalizers" (people who use few words in the
course of a day or a conversation) often become angry
when they are asked to express more than they already
have said. This leads them to argue from their feeling
base: "Why do you always make me feel bad?" "You're
mean." "You don't respect my feelings." They might
raise their voice and repeat the same sets of feelings or
thoughts over and over and they are now arguing.

Instead, the "nonverbalizer" can share information
such as this: "I'm starting to get upset but it's because
I'm not able to put my feelings into words yet. I'm not
upset with you and I don't want to be, so let me ponder
this and let's talk again tomorrow about it."

Meanwhile, the "verbalizer" (people who share lots of
information . . . almost streams of information in communication) get upset and angry when others don't
respond in kind. Someone who communicates fifty out
of sixty minutes will feel the other person is "holding
back" or "covering up" or that they just don't care.

These things upset the "verbalizer" and, once upset,
as with all communication about to go wrong, emotions will get the best of the verbalizer and communication will deteriorate rapidly. Because the verbalizer is

able to deliver words in large volume and speed, the verbalizer also is more likely to be deemed argumentative when she gets upset. Her voice will rise and she will become angry.

The verbalizer needs to share her feelings now: "I'm starting to become angry because I feel as if you are not sharing with me what I'm asking you for. Am I reading you right?"

It's very important that the nonverbalizer not take this communication as "blaming," because the nonverbalizer is by definition someone who doesn't communicate as much and certainly not as quickly as a verbalizer.

What can you do if you are dealing with an argumentative communicator that you have to deal with?

1. Tell the person you don't enjoy arguing but that you will discuss options and ideas.

2. Tell the person you respect his/her point of view but disagree.

3. If necessary, tell the person that this subject is something you don't wish to continue discussing because it is personal or volatile. (This is okay for business, of course, but it is not going to do the trick in long-term relationships.)

4. Speak your point of view clearly and make clear what it would take for you to re-evaluate your point of view.

5. Ask the person, "Is being right more important

than your feelings?" (In other words, what is at stake? Safety? Life/Death? Some long-term issue? Or is it about whether you squeeze the toothpaste from the middle or the end?)

6. Suggest the person frame his comments in a more gentle fashion: "I know you aren't saying that to attack me. It just hurts when you say it that way."

7. Or: "Instead of yelling, allow yourself to speak calmly and then I'll be able to listen to you better."

8. Or: "If you stop calling me names when we talk, I'd be a lot less defensive. Deal?"

What can you do if you are an argumentative communicator?

1. Ask more questions.

2. Be interested in how the other people in your life came to believe and think what they think.

3. Be aware that not everyone perceives discussion, debate, arguing, and fighting in the same way. Find out what those important to you believe about each of these things.

4. Ask the important people in your life specifically how you can communicate with them to help them know you don't want to argue but rather to discuss.

5. Determine why you need to be "right" or make someone else "wrong" in heated communications.

6. Always think of your intention. If your intention is gentle, speak more quietly. People associate quieter tones and gentler intentions.

7. Show people you care in ways other than verbally so they know you care when you do argue.

8. If you find yourself getting into a heated discussion, ask the other person if he feels you are arguing or discussing. Ask what the difference would be for him.

9. Ask your friend/associate/partner how you can communicate without giving the appearance of arguing.

10. Be certain that you make clear your intention so it is not misunderstood!

Chapter Five

Criticism: Being So "Honest" It Hurts

Critic: a person who judges, evaluates, criticizes, or analyzes; a person who readily tends to find fault or make harsh judgments.

Criticism: attacking someone's personality or character, usually with blame, instead of a specific behavior.

Complaint: targeting a specific behavior instead of overall personality or character.

> *"Sticks and stones can break my bones,*
> *But words can never hurt me."*

Care to place a small wager on that? The best odds-makers in Las Vegas wouldn't touch that one with a ten-foot pole in their worst nightmares.

We've all heard that nursery rhyme time and time again, and most of us know far too well that words can and do indeed cause pain and rejection and can hurt us spiritually, emotionally, mentally, and physically.

Doctors may mend broken bones daily but modern

medicine and those who practice it still haven't, after eons of study, figured out to mend a heart that has been trashed and tossed aside or a spirit that has been broken and fractured by the "well-meant" critique or advice of someone close.

Maybe you know someone whose sense of self, their own internal view of who they are, has been damaged by words spoken to them and what they have allowed those words to mean in their life. Maybe you know that person very, very well.

Aaron gets into his first car accident two short months after getting his license. He calls his dad from the scene of the accident, assures him that no one is hurt, and breaks the news that the car totaled. "I knew I shouldn't have let you get your license so young," yells his dad. "You're just not a responsible enough person, you'll never amount to anything in life."

Words can hurt. They do hurt, and sadly we often allow them to become permanent sources of pain that we carry with us throughout our lives.

You may know the kind of words that I am referring to. The cutting remarks spoken in anger. The put-downs and ridicule. The unfair comparisons. Sarcasms and mockery. Those pearls of wisdom or advice, the "constructive criticism" that hurts deep in our souls. Those are the verbal actions.

But there are also several types of nonverbal criticisms that we consciously or unconsciously, whether we intend to or not, do everyday also. Such actions as not paying attention to someone when they are speaking, picking lint off our clothes while someone is speaking to us, staring out a window, becoming distracted, speaking over someone else, interrupting, daydreaming, putting them aside until a more convenient time, etc.

These are all ways of nonverbally letting someone know that *"what you have to say doesn't interest me"; "I have no respect for your opinion";"you don't count."* Even the simple act of ignoring someone tells him or her, *"You're not good enough for me to pay attention to."*

Whether it be verbal or nonverbal, intended or not, one fact about criticism remains true:

> *Criticism is the pretty green snake of life; it can look innocent and beautiful to one person and deadly to another.*

"I'm only telling you this for your own good." *"If I didn't tell you, who would?"*

"If I didn't love you so much, I wouldn't say this BUT . . ." *"If you were more like your brother . . ."*

"Are you normally this stupid or do you work at it?" "Can't you do ANYTHING right?"

Sound familiar?

Has someone you have known ever started out a sentence with the words, "Well, if you *really* want to know what I think"? And how often did you *really* want to know his or her opinion? You could probably count all those times on one hand and still have five fingers left over!

People many times express their opinions or critiques in the course of our day and mask them with a preface of "just being *totally* honest," or "because I love you." Many of them probably don't even realize or are aware that they are causing pain to the person they are speaking to. The truth is, the very words they speak carry a message far greater than they ever could realize.

We tend to want the acceptance, the approval of the people we are in contact with. The deeper the relationship with the person, the more they mean to us, the more we crave their recognition, their love, and their respect. When we are hurt by their words, it cuts us deeper than any knife ever could and has the potential to do more damage than physical weapons.

Many people label their words "constructive criticism" or "advice," but in reality there is a very, very fine line between constructive and destructive. And most of us know the difference between giving or receiving welcomed feedback and verbal abuse.

I (RS) know there have been times in my life when I've hurt my spouse, my children, parents, and friends with careless words that I spoke without thinking, or with those words that accidentally slipped out of my mouth in a moment of anger. Those times when my size $9^1/_2$ foot somehow seemed to make its way up and lodge itself in my mouth before I knew it.

They've all done the same thing to me. Not out of meanness or cruelty. We've all done it at some point and most of us regret putting our mouths in gear before our brains caught up with our thoughts. But there are classes of people who deliberately use words as weapons, with the intent of inflicting as much emotional injury as possible. The things they say don't just feel like a slap in the face; they feel like a knife twisting in the gut. Perhaps that old nursery rhyme should really read,

> *"My bones can heal from sticks and stones, But words hurt me forever."*

Using words as weapons for verbal warfare is a practice that is as old as human language, but we still don't give words the attention they deserve. While we may have made great advances in understanding the damage that mental, physical, and sexual abuse can do, many people have still not realized the damage that words can do to injure others, often inflicting deeper, more long-lasting wounds than perhaps with our fists.

Research studies have shown that criticism is the quickest way to both diminish a person's self-image and poison a relationship. No one enjoys being around a critical person. Whether those words come from our spouses or significant other, employer, friends, or even total strangers, we tend to shut down inside, shutting out the words that hurt us, and we stop listening.

> *It is easier to be critical than to be correct.*
> Disraeli

When someone criticizes us, we don't "hear" the words as an adult would but rather as a small child would interpret those words. Deep inside us, buried in the layers of our subconscious mind, lies that young child that virtually controls, or at the very least seriously influences, our thoughts and responses, our actions, our experiences and our definitions. We adults process language through our childhood filters and develop our meanings of those words based on our childhood experiences and beliefs about ourselves.

We experience and interpret criticism as attack. Depending on our disposition, when criticized we either fold and crumble before the words we perceive as harsh or we fight back in defense. When we fold, we may stand embarrassed and ashamed, mumbling apologies like chastened children before an angry parent reliving and believing the critical words as truth and internalizing our behavior, adding to the mountain of negative self-esteem and self-worth.

In the animal kingdom, often the best defense is a good offense, and the human animal is no different in respect to fighting back. An aggressive counterattack is a common response to criticism. The basic principle is that the best way to overcome looking or feeling small and vulnerable or under attack is to get angry, be fierce, look big, and criticize in return.

In this sense, the typical incident of criticism between two people has each feeling little and vulnerable inside but acting big and scary on the outside. In such a relationship, giving and receiving criticism tend to become reactive and retaliatory, such as: *"I am going to hurt you because you are hurting me."*

Over time, this cycle of repeated behavior could lead to the person formerly *receiving* the criticism becoming the aggressor in any given situation. The reactive cycle then becomes: *"I am going to hurt you BEFORE you can hurt me."*

The person with this type behavior pattern tends to

become withdrawn and even more self-critical, which manifests itself in even harsher critiques of others.

> *We should become very thoughtful of the opinions of others. After all, there can always be three sides to a controversy— yours, theirs, and the right one.*

UNDERSTANDING CRITICISM

Human beings are conceptualizers, storytellers, and thinkers. Our main communication medium is language. We are *meaning-making* machines. We *have to* place our stamp, our version or hallucination of reality on everything that enters our minds. We *have to* have a meaning, i.e., our interpretation of the event, in order to process the information so our minds can then take the appropriate actions.

We all begin constructing a story about life and our relationship to it almost from the moment we are born. In a sense, each of us not only *has* a story but also *is* the story.

We write our life script, our movie, in which we are the main character. We are the heroes. We get to choose the scenes, setting, and appropriate music for our theme song. Things happen to us—some good things, some bad things. We take actions. We witness events and outcomes. We make decisions, some good ones and some bad ones. We have good guys and bad guys. We draw conclusions. And then we weave it all into an ongoing, always consistent, never-ending narrative tapestry based upon our unique hallucination of reality around us.

The main theme of our story, our life script, is our sense of self—who we are or, better yet, who we *believe* we are. Our life script and who we become are heavily influenced by what we were told when we were young and what we chose to believe about ourselves at that time.

Were we told that we were smart or stupid? Lazy or hardworking? Are our siblings really better than us? Are we beautiful, handsome, or homely? Are we destined to be rich or poor? Are we supposed to act the role of the victim or the hero? Are we part of an elite group or a persecuted minority? A good person or a bad person? A winner or a loser?

When we were offered each of these views, which of these scenarios did we believe about ourselves at the time, accept as truth, and allow to be embedded in our young subconscious minds and become reality for us when we grew older?

WHERE CRITICAL BELIEFS ORIGINATE

When we were children, our world was typically very small; it consisted mainly of our parents, teachers, and other grownups that we automatically labeled as the authorities on this exciting new world we were born into. We were positive they knew what they are talking about. They *had* to know everything. They had seen it all, we thought; they had been there, done that, and their words must be right.

In this picture, it is only natural that we designed our stories, our scripts, about ourselves based on the definitions, examples, and influences that our parents, our teachers, and those other authority figures that we knew were right had given us. They provided our basis for our imagined strengths and weaknesses, whether or not those definitions were in our own best interests.

To better understand the impact of critical language on children, it is vital to understand that children hear and process language differently from adults. They take things more literally than adults and tend to believe without question, especially when those ideas and statements come from an authority figure. When we were young children, we didn't particularly have the intellectual maturity to question our evaluation of our parents, to let their words roll off us like water on a duck's back.

Example: We are 3 years old and just spilled orange juice all over our clothes at breakfast, and our stressed-out, late-for-work parents yelled, "Can't you drink that without making a mess of yourself?"

Typically, we didn't think: "You know, I think my parents' expectations of me are too high. They have placed upon me very unrealistic goals for the short time I've been on earth. I am only 3 years old. As a matter of fact, I would say that the majority of my fellow nursery school friends come to school with some portion of their breakfast on their shirt. So I am not going to let this bother me!"

Well, at least, *most* of us didn't think that any way.

As children, we accepted their evaluation of us. We didn't ask questions, we just obeyed. If they said we couldn't drink without making a mess, we must become that mess. Ironically, when we become our parents' negative projection, it is a form of "honoring our parents." A "good" child listens to what his or her parents tell them and accepts it as truth, often literally, and we are pre-programmed by our parents, teachers, and other authority figures to be "good" children.

When the grownup in our life says, "You are stupid," we accept that we are stupid. When they ask why we "can't do anything right," we accept our incompetence as a truism. When we are told that we are a "bad boy" or "bad girl," naturally we assume this must be true. We might even try harder to be good. But all the while we know deep inside in our hearts that we must be bad. After all, mother or father knows best, don't they?

Children haven't yet developed the critical faculty that allows adults to evaluate new information, rejecting or accepting it based on past experience. In their short lives they simply haven't accumulated the life experiences and definitions on which to base those decisions yet. Children are listening and watching, forming their little pictures of whom they are and how life is. And they generally believe what they are told literally, whether that picture is positive or negative.

How else could we convince them that a fat old man with a snow white beard wearing a red velvet suit and riding in a sleigh pulled by flying reindeer will come down their chimney (even if there ISN'T one) with a bag of presents just for them every December 25th— but *only* if they behave themselves the entire rest of the year? Wow, I'd love to meet the parents that came up with *THAT* story to make their kids behave.

In an ideal world, we would all find the right words to say exactly what we mean, be supportive and nurturing, monitoring our language and words for possible harm. But ours is not an ideal world. We are the overworked, underpaid, overstressed, unrecognized, fast-food, take-out, I-want-it-now-and-I-won't-wait,

stick-'em-in-front-of-the-T.V., terrorism-stuck genera-
tion, and we were taught to downplay the importance
of language.

As a result, many of us pass down the same kind of
negative linguistic style that our parents used to rear
us, especially when we lose our tempers even a little bit.
We revert to familiar patterns, playing out old scenarios. If it was good enough for us, it's good enough for
our kids. We didn't turn out so bad, did we?

This isn't meant to imply that our parents were bad
people. They just might not have been aware of what
they were really saying and how our minds interpreted
their words.

We may tell our children that they are lazy when we
want them to learn that hard work brings rewards. We
may tell them they are irresponsible when we want
them to take on responsibilities. We may tell them they
are selfish when we wish them to be generous.

If we are married or in a relationship, we may overlook
the reasons we fell in love with our partners and berate
the little things they do as "bugging us on purpose." We
react harshly to perceived indignities and find fault with
them. We allow ourselves to develop "hot buttons" that
are rooted in our past that we apply to our current partners, and then we lash out with criticism when we are
tired and stressed from our day and need a whipping
post on which to land our frustrations.

Dr. John Gottman, a University of Washington professor and author of *The Seven Principles Of Making Marriage
Work* (Gottman and Silver; Crown Publishing Group,
1999), is perhaps the pre-eminent scholar of human relationships. He has studied communication patterns in

married couples and is able to predict with 94 percent accuracy which ones will divorce. He has found that criticism is one of four distinct communication behaviors that leads some couples straight to divorce court if it happens often enough.

Another useful insight Gottman has found is that men have less physiological capacity for conflict than their wives; they are more easily overwhelmed by marital stress and find it harder to recover afterwards. Men typically withdraw emotionally while women use an argument to vent their feelings, he says. If she makes the mistake of criticizing or attacking her husband right from the start, the damage to the conversation is usually irreparable.

One technique to prevent emotions from becoming an all-out verbal assault is to aim for a "complaint" (targeting a specific behavior) rather than a "criticism" (attacking a person directly) when addressing problems, advises Gottman. "You forgot to take out the garbage" stings far less than "I hate you when you forget to take out the garbage! Why can't you remember to do it?"

By using this method, your partner is more likely to comply with the desired wishes.

In our research into what makes marriages work/not work, we have found that there are generally six prime signs of the health of the relationship.

Prime Signs of Relationship Health

✔ **Abrasive Start Up**—starting or beginning an argument or discussion with accusations, criticisms, or sarcasm. Conversations that begin this way seem to be doomed to not resolve issues.

PRIME SIGN

✔ **Criticism**—focusing blame, name-calling, and judgment rather than the specific behavior.

✔ **Contempt**—Contempt poisons the relationship by conveying disgust; sarcasm, cynicism, eye-rolling, name-calling, and mockery are all forms of contempt. This behavior leads to more conflict and is often fueled by long-standing negative thoughts about your partner.

✔ **Defensiveness**—Returning the verbal volley of hurt only serves to continue the cycle of criticism. This tends to escalate conflict very rapidly.

✔ **Shutting Down**—Sometimes called "turtle-ing," this is the act of not responding or shutting down, retreating from a partner. Sometimes referred to as "the silent treatment." This act only serves to escalate the argument.

PRIME SIGN

✔ **Emotionally Overwhelmed**—One person becomes overwhelmed with intense feelings and feels the only way to avoid those feelings is to retreat in the relationship. This leads directly to the person affected shutting down and retreating into himself or herself, very often bringing with them highly critical nonspoken observations and feelings about their partners. These feelings then fester internally, poisoning the relationship until the affected party "blows his/her pressure cooker," typically reacting to a small problem in a huge fashion, releasing all the pent-up emotions all at once.

PRIME SIGN

✔ **Body Language**—physiological or nonverbal critiques such as ignoring, mockery, eye-rolling, and distraction that can push people into "fight or flight" systems. This is not the state where active problem solving can be done.

PRIME SIGN

✔ **Failed Attempts at Damage Control**—You can have all of these indicators in your relationship but still be successful with repairing the damage. A simple "Let's take a walk" or a shared memory (GOOD ONES ONLY!) can repair the damage of an argument. This can be difficult because on some level you must take responsibility for yourself and your actions.

PRIME SIGN

✔ **Bringing Up the Past**—Couples/partners entrenched in past negativity will rewrite the future toward that negativity. Bringing up the past to be used again time after time in the future is one of the major causes of relationship failure.

Gottman also reveals significant male and female differences in marriage. Research shows that women tend to complain and criticize while males tend to retreat and withdraw. This is due in part to a man's tendency to hear criticism as contempt. This explains why a man's blood pressure surges higher than his partner's. He hears this negative criticism as contempt for who he is as a person, whereas she does not filter the negativity as he does.

In fact, it often takes only the arrival of or indication of criticism to begin to emotionally overwhelm most men. Men typically avoid emotional conflicts by going off by themselves, retreating from battle so to speak.

If you ask a male who has retreated from a conflict with his partner to describe his state of mind, he often says, *"I am trying not say something I'll regret later."* He thinks he's idling along in neutral and making things better even though his partner may interpret his silence as an act of hostility. She can't understand how a simple critique can affect a male in the way that it does because she doesn't get emotionally overwhelmed in the same way. She reacts when feeling unloved. He reacts when feeling disrespected. A vicious cycle results from the criticism-and-withdraw pattern.

This cycle may be described as *"emotional hearing."* Since research has shown that men and women hear and interpret criticism in different ways, the male may typically hear his partner's critique as disrespect. The Catch-22 of criticism-love-respect becomes: without love, a wife reacts without respect, and without respect, a husband reacts without love.

CRITICISM IN THE WORKPLACE

Early folklore hero Davy Crockett had a simple motto that he lived his life by: *"Make sure you are right, then go ahead."* Every one of us, just as every successful person you will ever meet in your lifetime, will sometime face moments of criticism. It's how you handle that critique, how you deal with the emotions that criticism brings, that will determine your success or failure.

No matter what your career involvement, the more successful you become, the more attacks on your character and criticism you will receive. The only people exempt from this rule of life are those who don't attempt to accomplish anything in their lives. These are the *only* ones to remain forever above criticism.

If someone who has vowed to stay "until death do us part" won't put up with criticism, it's no wonder why most employees won't either. Most employees who are under a constant barrage of criticism will eventually take their talents elsewhere, and companies are left wondering where their entire talent base has gone. As production rates begin to decline, stock prices begin to fall and stockholders begin to question company leadership.

The sad fact is that most companies, small and large, fail to recognize this cycle. As long as employees perceive that the rewards of their job are at least equal to the cost they endure, they will continue to come to work and do the best job they can. It's when managers become critical of their employees that not only morale but also production begins to decline. Lack of recognition and appreciation is a major complaint of most factory workers.

I once worked for a major airline manufacturer and can vividly remember a common saying amongst workers there:

> *Working here is like wetting your pants in a dark suit; it may feel warm, but nobody notices.*

I personally don't know of one person who enjoys being treated as just another faceless number and then criticized for a lack of enthusiasm. Criticism = lower morale = criticism = lower production = criticism. It's not only a Catch-22; it's a Catch-44! Harsh, severe, and/or repeated criticism of employees has also given rise to new levels of violence in the workplace.

Companies typically offer vast incentives to entice and retain their employees by dangling the proverbial carrots such as more vacation time, bonuses, and better job titles. In reality, simply reducing the amount of criticism and adding even a small amount of praise would go a long way in keeping employees happy and increase production values.

SCENE FROM A WORKPLACE:

Scenario: *You work for a large major corporation. The supervisor of your area is verbally criticizing and scolding you out in front of your peers for a small, overlooked mistake that you did that has cost your company a large sum of money. The name-calling, finger-pointing, laying of blame, and language that he/she is using is abusive, threatening, and demeaning, in your opinion.*

As you imagine listening to the words coming from your supervisor's mouth, in reality, there could be two entirely different versions of your personality listening to those words and interpreting them differently. One version could be shutting down, folding, and crumbling before the discipline, becoming invisible, accepting the harsh criticism as truth of one's character. The other version could be reacting defensively, pulling on the verbal battle fatigues and preparing for all-out war.

As you imagine this scene now, notice how it makes you feel. Notice which of the two different versions of "you" is the one who is listening? The adult who made the mistake, or the small child being scolded for not being "good enough"?

Sometimes as we are being critiqued we tend to disassociate from the present and return to a "familiar" time, to that childhood part of us that we feel just didn't quite measure up to the expectations of someone—our parents, teachers, our authority figures. Keep in mind that the word "familiar" has neither a positive nor a negative connotation; it is just a familiar place to which we return subconsciously.

When we return to that part of ourselves, we react to criticism just as when we were children. We roll our eyes, shake our heads, make faces, fidget, become distracted, imitate and mock behaviors in an exaggerated manner. All of this typically infuriates the person who is delivering the critique. This normally then quickly escalates into verbal warfare and leaves both parties shattered and wondering what just happened.

HOW TO GIVE AND RECEIVE CRITICISM (FEEDBACK) EFFECTIVELY

Mary Kay Ash was an entrepreneurial phenomenon, a housewife who started a simple home-based business and created an empire. She not only created high-quality beauty products but also offered in-home beauty makeovers that made her clients, typically other housewives, feel important, special, and beautiful. She used to say in her seminars that in her company *"we stack every bit of criticism between two layers of praise."*

Even after her death, Mary Kay Ash continues to influence her salespeople, directors, and employees. They are still zealous in their loyalty and commitment to a woman's simple philosophy of how to treat people with respect by making them feel good about themselves.

Through extensive experiments, psychologist B.F. Skinner found that the most effective way to get the behavior we want is through praise instead of criticism. Rewarding even small steps can pay off big in the long run. Because negative criticism is so damaging, Gottman says that you need to give at least **five** positive comments or gestures to outweigh a single negative one. (Still other research has found that praise should be given intermittently rather than automatically or it will be taken for granted).

Hurt/Angry Feelings=Defense=Retaliatory
Offence=Hurt/Angry Feelings

Some simple strategies for receiving criticism/feedback:

Emotions take over when we are criticized. The cycle of hurt/angry feelings = defense = retaliatory offence = hurt/angry feelings can get in the way of coping with a situation. Before dealing with this difficult situation, it is necessary to bring those feelings into balance. When the cycle begins to take place and we begin to search to find that balance, sometimes it's helpful to:

1. Take several long, deep breaths.

2. Ask for time ("I need a few minutes to think about that").

3. Exert a bit of energy by walking around the block, house, office, or building.

4. Decide whether or not the criticism is intentionally meant to hurt.

A few good indications of whether criticism is meant to hurt can be:

Destructive criticism is meant to:

✔ Hurt or humiliate

✔ Manipulate or control

✔ Blame or create guilt

✔ Get attention

Constructive feedback is meant to:

✔ Help improve

✔ Make us aware

✔ Express concern or caring

✔ Keep communication lines open

✔ Clear the air when there may be differences in opinion

✔ Motivate us to make positive change

Remember when pointing out a mistake by another person: always consider the person's feelings and viewpoint. Sometimes it helps to put yourself in his or her shoes. A story has been told that when the late comic and actor Milton Berle was dining with his wife, Ruth, in a Hollywood restaurant, a waiter inadvertently put too much pepper on her salad. Mrs. Berle tasted it and remarked, "Hmm. It needs more salad."

A research study by North Dakota State University in 1992 found three highly effective ways to deal with criticism:

✔ Distraction

✔ Admitting the Truth

✔ Asking for Feedback

Distraction:

When there is *absolutely no truth* to the criticism, the distraction technique can be a very useful tool to dissipate the receiver's reaction. This technique allows the critic to voice his/her opinion and calming reassurances that the receiver has heard the critic's words.

Distraction also allows the receiver to hear the critic's words without immediately becoming defensive or anxious. The receiver becomes a listener without trying to read the critic's mind to see why he/she has criticized them. It gives the receiver an extra few valuable seconds that allows them to decide what to say or do next.

The goal of distraction is to interrupt the critical cycle, to provide a break in the verbal texture of the conversation before it results in conflict. Later, in a calm moment, the receiver can decide whether or not to do something about the situation that provoked criticism. The result is that the receiver *chooses* to be unaffected by manipulative, unjustified criticism. The critic will probably stop because it is no fun throwing words as arrows if the receiver does not react.

Some possible responses:

"You could be right about that."

"What you say makes sense."

"Perhaps I could . . ."

Never allow yourself to get caught up in the *"Yes, but . . ."* cycle. The problem with using the "Yes, but . . ."

cycle is that the person doing the critique does not want to hear an excuse. "Yes, but . . ." may actually even encourage the critic to be even more critical.

Unjustified criticism

"You're always late."
"Every time I tell you something is wrong, you get mad."

Distraction response

"Perhaps I'm a bit late this time."
"You might be right. I don't like it when things go wrong."

Admitting the Truth:

This technique can be very effective when a critic has pointed out a real concern. The first thing to do when handling valid criticism is to accept it as true but not fall into exaggerated self-critique, self put-downs and negative self-talk. Avoid over-apologizing for the error.

Admitting the truth allows the receiver to accept his mistakes and faults without apologizing for them. Admitting the truth also allows the receiver to recognize mistakes as mistakes, without feeling like a bad person. When admitting the truth, the goal is to get past this mistake or barrier and get on with the task at hand. The truth can help heal relationships and enable the individual and group to become productive again.

Once the receiver accepts the mistake, he can then move forward rather than become bogged down in depression and self-criticism. Others will accept them as they are and see them as fellow human beings.

Some possible responses

"You are right. I didn't do that as well as I could have. I got busy and didn't plan it out carefully enough."

"Yes, I probably didn't think it through carefully, and now that I know another approach, I can correct it."

Avoid saying, *"I made a mistake, BUT . . ." The use of the word* "but" attempts to explain why the mistake was made. There are many varied reasons why mistakes are made. This is not the time to focus on past performance but rather focus on future behavior: *"I made a mistake, AND I plan to do better next time."*

Requesting Specific Feedback:

Requesting specific feedback is probably the most powerful technique to deal with valid criticism. When the receiver requests specific feedback from a critic, he focuses on the future instead of dwelling on the past. Through specific questions, one can identify how to move directly into action. It forces a critic to look at potential solutions instead of pointing out mistakes. This technique extends an invitation to the critic to be on the receiver's side and work together to improve the situation.

By requesting specific "useful" feedback, it then prompts the critic to provide more criticism for the receiver to hear and analyze. It also keeps the criticism directed at the behavior or action rather than opening the door for a personal attack on one's character. The receiver then asks questions to gain facts and elicit his/her feelings.

As the receiver gains information, they exhaust the critic's complaints. They uncover true feelings and discover common ground so they can talk about things upon which both parties agree.

The goal in requesting specific feedback is to move on to manageable, productive activity as soon as possible. This technique allows people to break the manipulative cycle of criticism and defensive behavior by improving communication and understanding.

It is important to be genuine when asking for more information. It is a mandatory need to use a neutral tone of voice, one that is neither overly loud nor extremely soft-spoken. Sometimes it is helpful to paraphrase what we think we hear to help the critic clarify his/her expectations.

Some possible responses

"What specifically did I do?"

"If you were in my shoes, what would you do?"
"Help me understand what you think the problem is."
"Could you give me an example?"
"Is there anything else you can think of?"
"Are there other ways I could improve my work?"

Giving Criticism:

Sometimes it becomes necessary to provide feedback

or critique. Here are fourteen guidelines for providing successful critique/feedback without conflict:

1) Criticize the person's behavior rather than his character. Mention the actual incident rather than making grand generalizations or just labeling them. Aim for the "complaint" rather than the "criticism." Direct your complaint at the action, not the person.

Wrong response: *"You're obviously stupid when it comes to money."*
Right response: *"You made a mistake last week with the checkbook."*

2) Make criticisms or feedback specific, never demeaning. First empathize, and then criticize.

Scene: Son or daughter loses his/her coat at school:

Wrong response: *"You're so forgetful you'd forget your head if it wasn't attached!"*
Right response: *"I'm sorry you forgot your coat this morning. What can we do so this doesn't happen again?"*

3) Be sure the behavior you're criticizing can be changed. Foreign accents, height, physical features, baldness, performance abilities, and many other things cannot always be changed.

4) Use "I" and "we" statements to stress that you want to work out the problem together, rather than making threats. Offer to help rectify the situation together.

5)   Make sure the other person understands the reason for your critique. Don't criticize when you are angry.

6)   Don't belabor the point. Make it short and sweet; no lectures. No need to repeat the point over and over and over and over . . .

7)   Be aware of nonverbal body language when critiquing. Taking a person aside in front of others, walking him or her into a corner or another room, and facial expressions or threatening voice tones can all communicate that you are really going to "chew butt" on that person. Is this the message you really want to convey? Personal management, whether in the business community or on the home front, by using fear and intimidation usually isn't very conductive to a lasting relationship.

8)   Avoid comparisons with other people. The individuals are unique unto themselves.

9)   Ask for a specific changes. Don't expect the other person to read your mind, and vague hints don't help the other person know exactly what you are asking for. Ask him for ideas about changing how he behaves, rather than just bringing up your own. Remember that advice is just that: it's your opinion of how or what someone should do.

10) Don't set a tone of anger or sarcasm. Both are counterproductive. Avoid mockery at *ALL* times; it only serves to escalate.

11) Show the person you understand his or her feelings. Always criticize in private, never in public.

12) If you're putting your criticism in writing, cool off before writing the critical letter, email or memo. Wait a day and reread your handiwork. Do you still feel the same way? If so, send away and be sure only the person it is intended for sees it.

13) Start off by saying something good. Remember the recipe: Layer a single criticism between two layers of praise.

14) At the end, reaffirm your support and confidence in the person.

Chapter Six

Hostility and Contempt

Criticism: Attacking someone's personality or character, usually with blame, instead of a specific behavior.

Hostility: To be antagonistic toward someone; pertaining to an enemy.

Contempt: Disapproval tinged with disgust; communication that is intended to insult; to show disdain for another who is considered vile or worthless.

Contempt and hostility are fueled by thoughts of the other person's incompetence or disgust. They are disgusting. You think they are stupid. How do you show this?

1) Labeling

"You're a jerk."
"You're a bitch."
"You're a bastard."
"You're an idiot."
"You're a fool."
"You're stupid."
"You are incompetent."

2) Nonverbally

Roll your eyes when the other person says something.
Sigh heavily while he/she is communicating something to you.
Turn your back on him while he is talking.
Walk away from him while he is talking.

3) Covert Insults and Humiliations Designed to Cause Real Pain in Others

"Even *Andy* could get that one right."
"If you *really loved* me, you'd *lift* a finger to help around the house."
"You don't even *care* about your kids."
"You were *never there* when we really needed you."
"*Any kindergartener* could figure that out, you moron."
"You have *serious psychological* problems."

Contempt Breeds Contempt

It's true that contempt breeds contempt. Remember the last time you were involved in one of these:

"What the hell are you doing?"
"You told me to clean my room!"
"I told you to get the living room cleaned up because we have company coming, THEN to clean your room."
"What's the difference, Mom? No one is coming for TWO hours."
"That's it. You have no respect. You are grounded."
He looks at her in disbelief. Sits on his bed. Stares at her.
"What are you looking at?"
"Nothing. You're crazy."

"You will not speak to your Mother that way. You are grounded for one month! Now get this place clean. NOW!"

What happened here?

The son was cleaning his room. He probably should have been cleaning the living room first to prepare for company but he probably didn't know **why** he should be cleaning the living room first.

Deep inside, the son felt put out that he had to clean his room and the living room. He didn't mess up the living room, after all. His toddling sister did. He doesn't even go near the living room.

Deep inside, Mom felt as if she was in a pressure cooker. Company coming in two hours and she has four hours of work to do. And this isn't just any company. This is hubby's new client. A big one. The house has to be perfect. Tonight the pressure is on to make a really positive impression.

This is an example of how most people communicate all day long. Here is the next morning at work:

"Why aren't you working on the Johnson account?"

"You told me to get the numbers for the Friedman account and the Johnson account updated today."

"I told you that Johnson is going to be here in TWO hours. Get her account done, THEN do the Friedman account. Does any of this make sense to you?"

"Both sets of numbers will be on your desk in the next hour."

"I want the Johnson numbers NOW."

"Fine." (She drops the Friedman file, grabs the Johnson file, and returns to her desk.) "Is there anything else?"

"No. Just get that file to me ASAP."

Deep inside, the office worker is feeling hurt and angry. She doesn't feel trusted. She doesn't feel as if her boss understands her competency level. She is angry that her boss felt it necessary to make a scene over NOTHING in front of the staff. The boss once again made her look bad for no reason. The file would have been done with no problem . . . and no time delay.

Deep inside, the boss felt that, once again, people just don't get it. The top priority item gets second billing. What if there was an emergency or a problem and there wasn't time to get the Johnson file done? Why don't people do things in the order that makes sense? This woman is as stupid as her son . . . except he's 12 and has an excuse. Why does she keep this worker on? Probably because MOST of the time she does a good job, but THIS is just ridiculous.

The office worker goes home. She thinks all the way home that her boss is such a bitch.

"She really thinks I'm an idiot," she mutters over the steering wheel. "I hate her. I am going to quit. I will not put up with this insanity any longer. I can't handle it. She always is on me. Why doesn't she just let me work and do my job?"

She pulls in the driveway. Husband is home. "Hope he had a good day," she says again over the steering wheel. She goes in. They hug, kiss, sit down, and say hello for a minute.

"How was your day?"

"Oh, it was okay. I'm sick of that witch, though."

"Did she say something again?"

"Yes, she was sticking her nose in my business again."

"You know, next time she does that you should just tell her to leave and let you get your work done."

"It's not quite that easy. She *is* the boss ya know."

"I know that but that doesn't give her a right to be so overbearing. Tell her that you are good at what you do and that you don't need her meddling."

"She's so in your face, very intimidating (kind of like you, honey, now that I think of it), and I don't want to push the wrong button and lose my job."

"Geez, they can't fire you for doing your job and saying how you feel. Don't let her push you around."

"I'll take care of it." (I have no idea how but I don't want to talk about this anymore. Now I feel incompetent here too!)

"Good. If you don't let it fester you can have it taken care of tomorrow and never deal with it again."

"That's easy to say. You are the supervisor at your office. I'm just a peon."

"I respect people who speak their mind as long as they are respectful."

"She doesn't respect anyone but herself. She is not you."

"I know. I just hate to see you pushed around."

"I can handle myself." (No I can't. Why do I say things like that?)

"OK, honey. Keep me posted." (I'm not going to make her feel bad by continuing this.)

Solutions for Contempt and Hostility

Hostility is attacking someone with the intent to do

verbal harm. Some people simply fly off the handle and criticize others. As we discussed earlier, that has to be stopped. Others will complain about behaviors of their partners. That isn't so bad in the long run, though it isn't exactly a recipe for happiness. What is among the worst offending sins that is detrimental to the soul is communication with the intent to harm, whether in public or private.

If you or your partner are intentionally communicating with the intent to harm, you must stop immediately. Hostility is something that no soul should be involved in. There is no benefit in hostility for anyone. The desire to harm others through communication is a sign of serious relationship problems that need to be corrected as soon as possible.

If your partner is intentionally communicating with you in a hostile manner, you need to gently share this information with him at the first reasonable moment. The partner should be allowed to communicate his feelings about the reason for his hostility and then move to a solution. The solution is not the silent treatment but increased communication. However, as you deal with the specific issue of hostility do not bring up all the relationship problems of the past. This only gives cause to do the exact opposite of your goal.

What model of communication would you propose? Propose it. Get agreement if appropriate and start communicating with the intention of making each other feel good about the other. The exercises on the coming pages will help you rebuild a relationship that was on treacherous ground.

ELIMINATING HOSTILITY IN RELATIONSHIPS

Hostility and contempt in personal relationships (and all relationships are personal to some degree) need to be dealt with immediately. Hostility and contempt are relationship killers. Will the relationship end, or will love be recreated? If it's time to start over, do so now. The following plan for recreating your relationship will be of great help. Here's how:

> *Design a completely safe environment in which you and your partner may communicate.*

If you have been hitting your partner, change your behavior. Changing your emotions will happen later, but change your behavior now! Your partner was hit as a child. If you tend to blow up at your loved one, stop now. She was yelled at as a child. If you get up and leave when you are angry, stop it now. She was abandoned as a child, and you're acting just like the parent.

Think carefully about these examples before moving on to number two. Create an atmosphere where it is safe to talk and communicate. Promise each other that this is a time to listen and not judge, evaluate, or point fingers. Create an atmosphere where you can experience positive communication.

> *Describe three things that you can implement in your relationship today to create a safe environment for yourself and your partner in which to communicate.*

Stop all criticism immediately!

There is no such thing as constructive criticism to the parts of the unconscious mind that are attempting to finish their childhood!

Create sessions of healing acceptance.

Healing acceptance sessions occur when you and your partner sit down and talk just as if you had been hit by a car in an accident. You want to find out if the other person is all right and see what you can do for him/her. You need to tell your partner that you want him to acknowledge what you are about to tell him without rebuttal or explanation on his part.

No defensiveness is necessary. You are simply telling him that you are wounded and that it hurts. You will not blame him. You will use statements such as, "I feel ..." and "I hurt ..." He should say, "I understand," and "What else do you want to tell me?" "Go on." "Okay." Those four statements and questions are the sum of what the non-injured partner will say.

It is vitally important never to attack your partner during these "healing acceptance" sessions. Keep it open and loving, and then your relationship will be on its way forward!

Perform random acts of kindness for your partner.

A wonderful tool to foster communication with others is by performing a random act of kindness. Bring a card or gift home after work. A small and inexpensive gift shows your thoughtfulness and can do wonders for your relationship in a big way. Notice the key word is "random." It means unpredictable. Be unpredictable with your times of giving.

Do something that you normally don't do around the house. If you never do the dishes, do them one night. If you never cut the lawn, cut it. The unexpected can be very pleasant and very appreciated.

> *Return to a successful ritual you liked.*

Was there something special you did while you were dating? Do it now.

> *Express your love and feelings for your partner with hugs, kisses, and verbal affirmations of love, often.*

Most people need to be hugged and kissed. Leo Buscaglia used to prescribe at least a dozen hugs per day for the maintenance of a relationship. Saying "I love you" may get old after 30,000 recitations, but you never hear of anyone complaining that their partner tells them that they love them too often!

(By the way, I wouldn't recommend this in the office

environment, as the corporation by mandated law has become a cold and thus difficult place in which to communicate.

Discover his/her needs and wants while sharing yours.

For you to have a wonderful relationship, discover what your partner currently loves about your relationship. Then ask your partner what he thinks could improve your relationship. Ask your partner the questions below, in the Successful Relationship Elicitation exercise. (Don't do this all in one sitting!)

This exercise will help you discover what is important to your partner and will help you transform your relationship.

SUCCESSFUL RELATIONSHIP ELICITATION

The following questions are to be used as discovery tools for you and your partner to learn more about each other and deepen your bond. Use these questions as tools to gently start to help you and your partner "peel each other's onions."

The first questions will help you and your partner build resources to which you can refer in tough times. Later questions help discover weaknesses and areas that need change or improvement. Spend about twenty minutes for each partner with these questions, over several days.

- What is the best thing about our relationship?
- What else?

- What do you believe you should learn about me to improve our relationship?
- What do you think I should learn about you to improve our relationship?
- What are two things I do that annoy you?
- What are two things you do that you think annoy me?
- How happy are you with our sex life?
- What can I do to make our sex life more intoxicating?
- What would you be willing to do to make our sex life more intoxicating?
- When we argue from now on, should we agree to kiss and make up before the argument gets out of hand?
- What will our "cue" be for this to happen?
- What do you do around the house that you think I don't appreciate?
- What do you do at work that you think I don't appreciate?
- What do I do that you probably don't appreciate as much as you could?
- What do you want to know about my past that I haven't told you?
- What do you want me to know about your past that you haven't told me?
- When should I be jealous?
- When do you think you should be jealous?
- How can we go from having a good relationship to having a fantastic relationship?

These questions allow us to discover more about our partner in a couple of hours than we may have discovered in years. Questions are an under-used element of communication in our culture. Beginning to ask gentle questions will put you on the track to improving communication and thereby improving your relationship no matter how good or bad it already is.

Learning what is important to your partner and being certain your partner understands what you need and want makes having a good relationship much easier. This elicitation helps you take the guesswork out of knowing what helps the other person feel more at ease with you.

The result? Hostility and contempt float away and healthy mature communication is fostered.

Chapter Seven

Ignoring Nonverbal Communication: Yours . . . Theirs

Most social psychologists will tell you that nonverbal communication makes up about two-thirds of all communication between two people or between one speaker and a group of listeners. Yet, almost nothing is written about body language. No one teaches you how to communicate nonverbally with others. No one shows you how to read the body language of other people. No one shows you how to utilize the space around you to communicate with others.

Being unable to decode nonverbal communication is like listening to the news on the radio and hearing only three out of every ten words that are spoken. You will misunderstand what you hear and you will be frustrated by the experience.

In this chapter you will learn how to watch for important cues from other people's nonverbal communication. You will also learn to intentionally utilize the space around you to convey messages that you want communicated. Finally, you will learn how to present yourself and to communicate with your body so that you are understood by others, both at the conscious and unconscious level of thinking.

THE TALKING BODY

Some people just sit there when they talk. Their eyes don't light up, their hands never leave the table, their voice never rises or falls. They are not interesting and are not going to be the focus of anyone's attention.

People who are exciting, intense, and fun move. The most charismatic people of the twentieth century were people such as Elvis Presley and Marilyn Monroe. When they moved the world watched.

Does your face move when your mood changes? Does your body move as you become excited? If not, start paying attention to people who are drawing the positive attention you desire and see what they are doing right! Generally speaking people who subtly move while they talk (hands, arms, facial expressions) are considered more expressive and are easier to communicate with because they are perceived as more likable.

CAN YOU HEAR YOUR BODY TALKING?

You have less than ten seconds and realistically closer to four seconds to make a good first impression on those with whom you come in contact. There is a world of research that clearly indicates that you will be judged professionally and personally in the first few seconds of your meeting someone for the first time. In fact, your first impression is recorded and is used as a yardstick for all future communication by those you meet. Whatever that first impression is going to be on your part, you want it to be intentional, on purpose.

Before going any further in discussing verbal communication, we had better take a look at how to increase "liking" with your body language. Most people are completely unaware of just how much their body says and how it often contradicts what the words are saying!

There are numerous elements of what we call body language. They include your physical features, both changeable and unchangeable, your gestures and signals you send to others at the conscious and unconscious level, and the space that you use when communicating with others. In this chapter we will touch on all of these important areas of body language.

WHAT YOU LOOK LIKE REALLY TALKS

Let's begin with your physical appearance. Here are some astounding facts that will give you pause for thought when you consider how important appearance is in attraction.

Recent psychological research has revealed that college students who look at a two-second video clip of a professor teaching can predict how students who spend an entire semester with that professor will like that professor by the end of the semester. In other words, a student watching a two-second clip of someone says, "I like him." Or "I don't like him." That statement is then recorded with other students viewing the two-second clip.

At the end of the semester, students who have taken a class with the professor anonymously record whether or not they liked the professor. With incredible accuracy, those watching the two-second clip predict what the entire class will feel at the end of the semester. It sounds unbelievable but it is true. One of the big mistakes we make is making a poor impression on others.

THE POWER OF PHYSICAL APPEARANCE

Did you know that in university settings professors who are considered physically attractive by students are considered to be better teachers on the whole than unattractive professors? Attractive professors are also more likely to be asked for help on problems. These same attractive professors also tend to receive from other students positive recommendations to take their classes and also are less likely to receive the blame when a student receives a failing grade! (Romano and Bordieri, 1989)

Did you know that marriage and dating decisions are often made with great weight placed on physical attractiveness? A wide variety of research indicates that men will often reject women who are lacking (in their opinion) in positive physical features. Women, on the other hand, place less significance on a man's physical attractiveness in considering him for a date or marriage. (Studies by R.E. Baber)

Did you know that in studies done on college campuses, it has been proven that attractive females (attraction as perceived by the professors) receive significantly higher grades than male students or relatively unattractive females? (Studies by J.E. Singer)

Among strangers, individuals perceived as unattractive in physical appearance are generally undesirable for any interpersonal relationship! (Studies by D. Byrne, O. London, K. Reeves)

In one significant study of fifty-eight unacquainted men and women in a social setting we learned that after a first date, 89 percent of the people who wanted a second date decided on the basis of the attractiveness of the partner! (Brislin and Lewis)

When communicating, attractive females are far more convincing than females perceived as unattractive. (Mills and Aronson)

In yet another study, we find that young men who are obese are generally considered to be slothful and lazy. Both men and women who are obese are generally perceived to have personality characteristics that place them at a disadvantage in social and business settings. (Worsley, 1981)

You probably haven't considered that how you present yourself to others is important in how they will like you and communicate. That is another mistake. People both unconsciously and consciously notice what you look like and how you present yourself. They judge this unconsciously and then filter everything you say through that judgment.

CAN YOU CHANGE YOUR APPEARANCE?

Study after study reveals that how you look is critical to someone's first impression (and every impression thereafter!) of you. So what can you do to change how you look? You can't change everything about your physical appearance but you can definitely make changes that will give you a booster shot.

Research studies tell us that the "exposure principle" increases our "face value." Specifically, the exposure principle says that the more often you are seen by someone the more attractive and intelligent you appear to them. If you weren't gifted with a Cindy Crawford or Tom Cruise face then it's time for you to take advantage of the exposure principle.

If you don't have the advantage of being "seen" time

after time by a person or a group, then you must make the most of what you have. In other words, you want to look as good as you possibly can on every given day. Because of the significance of body image, energy level, and weight, you must do what you can to keep your body weight down and your body in shape for your overall perception to be as good as it can be.

Your teeth will tell a tale as well. If your teeth are yellow and look like you just ate, your face value is obviously greatly reduced. Do everything you can to keep your teeth pearly white and you will be perceived as more attractive. (You've already seen the communication benefits of the perception of attractiveness.)

When you watch the news tonight on television, look at the teeth of every news anchor, weather person, and sports announcer. They all have beautiful white teeth. There's a reason for that, and that is positive impression management. We tend to believe and like people more when they appear competent.

WHERE YOU SIT CAN CHANGE HOW PEOPLE LOOK AT YOU!

Communicating in business? Standing in someone's office is a problem that will need an immediate solution. As soon as pleasantries are exchanged, you and your customer should be seated. If you are both standing for an extended period of time and your customer doesn't have the forethought to offer you a chair, then you can ask, "Should we sit down and be comfortable?" Unless you are in a retail environment, sales are not made and deals are not negotiated standing up.

You may have an option of considering where to sit. If so, you are in luck. Scientific research is on your side in telling you exactly where to sit. Seating options normally occur on lunch or dinner dates at a restaurant and in meeting rooms. If you are in a restaurant, quickly search out (with your eyes) a location that allows you to sit facing the majority of the people in the restaurant so your client is obligated to sit facing you, away from the clientele and staff of the restaurant. This is ideal for booth seating.

Your partner's or client's attention should be on you, not the waitress, bus boy, and the dozens of other people in the restaurant. Your seat selection will assure you his attention. Once you have the attention of your customer, only you can make your presentation or engage in conversation.

HOW DO YOU SELECT SEATING?

Ideally, you can create a seating arrangement that is most likely to facilitate the communication process. Here are the key rules in seating selection:

1) As a rule, if you have already met your client or friend once and you know he is right-handed, attempt to sit to his right. If she is left-handed, sit to her left.

2) If you are a woman attempting to communicate effectively with another woman, sitting opposite of each other is as good or better than sitting at a right angle.

3) If you are a woman and want to help a man feel comfortable, the best option is to be at a right angle if at all possible.

4) If you are a man attempting to communicate effectively with another man, you should be seated across from each other in the booth setting if possible. (However, research also shows that men actually communicate better at right angles than straight across from each other in close quarters.)

5) If you are a man attempting to communicate well with a female in business or in a social setting, you should be seated across from her at a smaller, more intimate table.

WHAT DO YOU DO ONCE YOU ARE SEATED?

Waiting for the waitress to come in a restaurant can be awkward if you do not know your date or your client very well. If you are meeting your client in her office, you will immediately get down to business after brief pleasantries. (It should be noted that sometimes pleasantries do NOT have to be brief. Many of my biggest and best presentations were made in the last two minutes of meetings that would extend to two hours discussing everything from baseball to sex to religion. The level of rapport and quality of mutual interests will ultimately be your guide.)

Once seated, keep your hands away from your face and hair. There is nothing good that your fingers can do above your neck while you are meeting with a client. The best communicators in the world have wonderful and intentional control of their gestures. They know, for example, that when their hands are further from their body than their elbows that they are going to be perceived in a more flamboyant manner.

While you are seated, if you are unfamiliar with your

date or client it is best that you keep both feet on the
floor. This helps you maintain control and good body
posture. People who are constantly crossing and uncross-
ing their feet and legs are perceived as less credible, and
people who keep one foot on their other knee when talking have a tendency to shake the free foot, creating a silly
looking distraction. Feet belong on the floor.

Meanwhile, your hands will say a great deal about
your comfort level. If you are picking at the fingers of
one hand with the other, you are sending an unconscious message that shows fear or discomfort. This is
picked up by the unconscious mind of the customer
(or your friend) and makes her feel uncomfortable.

If you don't know what to do with your hands and
you are female, cup your right hand face down into
your left hand, which is face up. Don't squeeze your
hands. Simply let them lie together on your lap.

For men, the best thing to do is to keep your hands separate unless you begin to fidget, at which point you will follow the advice of your female counterpart, noted above.

HOW CLOSE IS TOO CLOSE?

Whether seated or standing, you should stay out of
your client's "intimate space." Intimate space is normally
defined as an 18-inch bubble around the entire body of
your client. Entering this space is done at your own risk.

This doesn't mean that you can't share a secret with
your date or your client. This doesn't mean you can't
touch your date or your client. It does mean that if you
enter into "intimate space," you are doing so strategi-
cally and with a specific intention. There can be great

rewards when entering intimate space but there are also great risks, so be thoughtful about your client's "space."

Similarly, if you leave the "casual-personal" space of a client, which is 19 inches to 4 feet, you also stand at risk of losing the attention of the client. Ideally, most of your communication with a new customer should be at the 2-to-4-foot distance, measuring nose to nose. This is appropriate, and generally you begin communication at the 4-foot perimeter of space and slowly move closer as you build rapport with your client.

WHAT IS EFFECTIVE EYE CONTACT?

Eye contact is critical in any face-to-face meeting. As a rule of thumb, you should maintain eye contact with your business client two-thirds of the time and a date about 80 percent of the time. This doesn't mean that you look at her eyes for twenty minutes then away for ten minutes. It does mean that you keep in touch for about seven seconds then away for about three seconds, or in touch for about fourteen seconds and away for about six seconds.

Eye contact doesn't mean just gazing into the eyes. Eye contact is considered any contact in the "eye-nose" triangle. If you create a triangle from the two eyes to the nose of the customer, you create the "eye-nose" triangle. This is the area that you want for 65-70 percent of eye contact.

Should you sense that your client is uncomfortable at this level, reduce your eye-contact content. Many who were born and reared in the Eastern countries (Japan, for example) are not accustomed to the eye contact that Americans are.

Eyes are a fascinating part of the human body. When a person finds someone or something very appealing to him, his pupil size (the black part of the eyes) grows significantly larger. This is one of the few parts of body language that is absolutely uncontrollable by the conscious mind. You simply cannot control your pupil size.

If you are interested in someone else, your pupil size will grow dramatically. If someone else is interested in you, their pupils will grow larger when looking at you, and there is nothing they can do about it. This is one of the powerful predictors of liking in nonverbal communication.

It should be noted that pupil size will also get larger in situations of extreme fear and when a setting is dark. Pupils expand to let more light in and, like a camera, when the setting is very well lit the pupils will contract to the size of a very tiny little dot.

If you follow the tips in this chapter for improving your impression on others, being careful about appropriate dress as to the setting and event and careful with your use of space, you will be perceived as more capable, intelligent, and even attractive in personal relationships and in business. More importantly, you help set others at ease.

There are two other telling behaviors relating to the eyes.

First, if someone is blinking far more rapidly than they normally do, that is usually an indicator of annoying lighting in the setting you are in or of anxiety and/or lying on the part of the person.

Second, if you are in conversation with someone and his/her eyes are easily distracted by the goings on in the environment, this is usually a good indicator that you haven't earned the interest of your listener. In general, it is a very wise strategy for you to keep your eyes well trained on your date or business associate in distracting environments. To constantly look around at the environment when you are with someone else is perceived as rude. To keep eye contact with another person instead of being distracted by extraneous activity is considered flattering and complimentary, especially by women.

THE EYES HAVE IT

As I noted above, you know that you are able to get a pretty good idea of how someone feels about you by looking at their eyes. You get even more information about how someone feels about you when you put that "look" into the context of his/her facial expression and body language.

Did you know that women initiate about 65 percent of all flirtatious encounters with men? Usually this is done with their eyes. How you look at someone can be perceived as seductive, frightening, caring, loving, bored, secretive, or even condescending. The eyes reveal a great deal about what is going on inside of us. If you can learn how to look and send the right message at the right time with your eyes you will be perceived as more attractive by more people.

There are six basic emotions in the human experience and the eyes capture them all. There are many more than six different emotions, but most of the emotions we experience are a combination of the six basic emotions. By simply looking at a person's eyes we can tell whether they are experiencing happiness, surprise, disgust, fear, anger, or sadness.

Think about that. Across the world people are the same in this respect. We all show the six basic emotions in the same fashion. The eyes are amazing windows to the emotions we all experience. By paying close attention to the eyes we can learn a great deal about people and, in particular, those we wish to attract.

It is a true statement that most people will judge others in the first two or three seconds after their first meeting. Therefore, doesn't it make sense to have them hypnotized by your eyes and your understanding of their wants and needs? How do you do this? You use your eyes in simple yet powerful ways to build rapport and create feelings of arousal in the person you are attempting to communicate with. To do this you need only to apply the key ideas you will learn in this chapter.

I (KH) recently had laser surgery on my eyes to improve my vision without glasses. In the screening process, I learned that some people shouldn't have the surgery because their pupils dilate (get bigger and blacker!) to a size that is abnormally large.

Everyone's pupils dilate when it is darker in the environment, and they contract when it is lighter. When the sun is shining brightly in your eyes, your pupils will be at their smallest. When you walk into a dark room, your pupils will be at their largest. The pupils get larger to gather more light. This helps the eyes see more of what is in the environment.

Your pupils will also get larger when you are terrified. There is an evolutionary response in your body that helps you collect more information about an experience that is frightening. The senses all sharpen in moments of great fear. Your hearing becomes more acute, your sense of touch is enhanced, and you can even taste fear. The pupils in your eyes get larger. This helps bring more light in even if the environment is already well lit. Your brain needs that information to help you escape and to protect you from danger.

Everyone's pupils dilate to a different maximum size, and everyone's pupils have a slightly different normal state. However, there is one amazing fact about those eyes: When someone looks at you and their pupils get big and black, they are either scared to death of you or they like you!

It's almost impossible to control the increase in pupil size that occurs when we see something we like. This expansion is also an evolutionary process that happens to take in more of something that is very dear to the person. Unfortunately for the observing person, it is an uncontrollable response.

Recent research into pupil dilation has proven quite interesting. A researcher showing pictures of a baby to women results in pupil dilation in the majority of women. Women viewing pictures of a baby with the mother elicits an even greater pupil-dilation response. These same women viewing a beautiful landscape experience an enlarging pupil size as well.

Interestingly, women viewing a picture of an attractive man, on average, don't experience quite the size of pupil dilation noted in the above scenarios! Women can be impressed by a man's appearance, but at least at an evolutionary or biological level, physical appearance isn't going to turn on every woman who passes. (Just what does turn women "on" will be discussed later in this book!)

These same researchers took the picture of that same beautiful baby and showed it to men. The men's response was a non-event. Their pupils, on average, didn't dilate. When viewing the baby with the mother, there was again a non-event. Generally speaking, nothing happened. When the men were shown pictures of a beautiful landscape, again, nothing happened. As soon as a man was shown a photo of a beautiful woman, the pupils, on average, dilated to a big and black orb. A man, it would appear, is very much "turned on" by the sight of a beautiful woman, or even a picture of one.

Pupil dilation in women, when in the presence of real live men, is another matter. Women typically are not visually aroused by photographs in the same way that men are. Women are very stimulated by some men in some contexts. When women are sitting across from men who arouse them, their pupils do dilate. To the observant witness, it is obvious. Most people are oblivious to the enhanced pupil size and yet it is one of the most telling signals of attraction.

As a public speaker, I (KH) have spoken to hundreds and hundreds of audiences all over the world. As I speak, I am aware of the women whose eyes are big and black, and I always address my presentation to them, making eye contact with those who appear to be most interested in me and/or what I'm saying. They don't know this is why I selected them to make eye contact with (at least they didn't until now).

Part of my job is to excite and inspire an audience

when I speak. Therefore I need to gain as much rapport with the audience as I can. By making contact with the people who like me the most, I am able to gain agreement from those people. They nod their heads, lean forward, show interest, and smile, and everyone in the audience sees how much fun they are having. In groups, head nods are like a virus. Once one person nods his head almost everyone does!

I receive all of this positive feedback in part because I don't just look at faces in an audience. It is because I look at the eyes of dozens of people in the audience and find the biggest pupils I can locate! These searches are like a treasure hunt that always has a pot of gold at the end. If I can do this with an audience of 50 or 100, can you imagine how easy this is to do in a smaller group at a party or in a public place? Start paying attention to the eyes that are looking at you.

You may wonder, "What if you are wrong? What if those eyes are just big because they are among the women whose eyes are normally large?" Then aren't you just fooling yourself into believing that all of those people like you?

My response is, "Of course." When you hallucinate, it should always be something that increases your self-esteem and self-confidence!

A little while back there was a fascinating study that revealed that when you show two pictures of the same woman to a man, the man will perceive the picture of the woman with the biggest pupils to be significantly more attractive. Many magazine cover editors know this and actually touch up the cover picture. Obviously, in the bright light of a photographer's studio the subject's pupils would be very small. Because of the importance of pupil size and attraction, the model's pupils are made much larger than they possibly could be. This makes the final picture irresistible to the magazine purchaser. We simply love people with big eyes!

EYE CONTACT

Men often ask, "How can you tell when a woman is interested in you?" My response is simple. "If you see her give you one glance, she saw you. If she looks back in less than a minute, she finds you attractive."

Men will stare at women for thirty minutes and never have their gaze reciprocated. Meanwhile, every woman in the environment can see whom the man is interested in and direct their attention elsewhere! Women, on the other hand, are more intuitive about eye contact. They will look around a room and see who is there. They will give second glances to those they are attracted to and avoid men they are not interested in.

When eye contact is made, it is a good idea to give someone "an eyebrow flash." This is a quick "raising" of your eyebrows that lets the other person know you are attracted to and interested in them. The eyebrow flash is common to every culture on earth. People who do not reciprocate with an eyebrow flash are sending a message that they are not interested. Make sure if someone "flashes" you that you flash back!

After the flash has happened, you will find it uncomfortable to maintain eye contact with that person for more than a few seconds. Therefore, break your eye contact after a few seconds. Look down and then back again at the person you are interested in. Look down,

not up. Looking up is usually a sign of not being interested in the other person, so be careful not to do that!

The eyebrow flash is also a useful communication
technique for people you know well. Sometimes you
can be communicating with a friend and you have no
idea if they are on the same page as you are. Are they
with you? The eyebrow flash can snap them out of their
trance and bring them back to the present.

Eye Contact in Intimate Settings

The amount of eye contact and the type of eye contact we have with another person are important.
Consider intimate settings. Women have a variety of
responses to lengthy eye contact. Most women love to
be the only person a man will look at in a room. They
want undivided attention and are aroused when they
receive it. However, there are a percentage of women
who have a fear of being dominated or being harmed
by men.

These fears usually stem from a time when they were
younger. They may have been harmed or abused by a
man. These women do not feel comfortable with
lengthy eye contact. Therefore what helps one woman
feel comfortable and cared for will quickly create discomfort in others.

Men on the other hand tend to find exclusive eye
contact very arousing. Men rarely have fears related to
eye contact when they are with a woman they like. Men
and women both want to be the center of the other
person's world. In fact, the most charismatic and
charming people are those who can make the world
melt away around another person. What does the

research show about enhancing communication effectiveness with eye contact?

Use the 70 percent rule in the United States: 70 percent of the time you will look at the other person in the "eye triangle." This triangle extends from the ends of the eyebrows to the tip of the person's nose.

If you are with someone whom you are in an intimate relationship with or are pursuing one with, you can make this wonderful visual voyage. Caress your partner with your eyes as you gaze in this triangle. When you break eye contact, do not break to look at another person. Keep your focus of attention with this person. When you intentionally break your eye contact, do so by looking down, to the left, or to the right. Looking up in response to a question or while telling a story is just fine, but looking up to break eye contact is often thought of as a sign of waning interest!

Another way to break eye contact is to move your eyes outside the triangle and move your eyes to the person's hair, compliment the person (only women in this case) on how nice her hair looks, and then return to her eyes. On a first date, a man should use what I call the "shoulders rule." A man should gaze only at what appears above the shoulders on a first date. In business, this is obviously a must. Women spend two to ten times more time getting ready to go out.

In business or in pleasure, men desperately want eye contact with women. Men gauge the interest of a woman by her eye contact. Men are very competitive and territorial when it comes to women looking at other men. They see this as a sign that the woman is no longer interested in them, or that the interest is fading. Therefore, if a woman wants to continue to attract the man, the woman needs to maintain steadfast eye contact. A man's self-esteem will crumble if a woman begins to observe all the male competition when in the presence of a man. This is true in business or in pleasure.

On the other hand, we can safely predict that if we have the full attention of the one we are with, he/she holds us in esteem to some degree. There is no other indicator that is as powerful as eye contact that can show interest in another person. Our eyes unconsciously and automatically move toward that which interests or arouses us. We all know that and we all judge our value in some part by the response we receive from other people.

How does eye color cause changes in communication?

In communication it's always a mistake to assume that little things don't matter. After all, it's obvious now that you think about it, to look good when communicating. But it would be ridiculous to think that things that are completely beyond our control, such as eye color, could matter in communication.

Think Cameron Diaz looks sweet? Vanessa Williams is sexy? Julia Roberts seems intelligent? It may be due to their eye color, according to a recent survey conducted by CyberPulse*, a division of Impulse Research Corporation in Los Angeles. The study found that people often associate different eye colors with specific personality traits. The survey also determined that it may be possible for individuals to influence people's perception of them simply by changing the color of their eyes with colored contact lenses.

The personality trait that respondents of the study most associated with brown eyes was intelligence (34 percent of respondents said so). Brown-eyed people were also thought to be trustworthy (16 percent said this), and kind (13 percent). Qualities they least associated with brown-eyed individuals were shyness (6 percent) and creativity (4 percent).

Survey results showed that blue-eyed individuals are most often seen as exuding sweetness (42 percent), and being sexy (21 percent) and kind (10 percent), but not shy (4 percent), or trustworthy (2 percent). In contrast to brown eyes, blue eyes are not typically associated with being smart as only 7 percent of respondents thought of blue-eyed people as intelligent.

Twenty-nine percent of respondents associated green eyes with sexiness. Green-eyed people are also thought of as creative (25 percent) and a little devious (20 percent). Like their blue-eyed counterparts, they are not considered trustworthy (3 percent) or shy (3 percent), but in contrast, people with green eyes are not thought of as sweet (only 4 percent of respondents associated green eyes with being sweet).

Of the respondents, 60 percent expressed an interest in changing their eye color. More respondents would change their eye color to green (27 percent) than to any other color. In second place, 26 percent of those surveyed said that they would change their eye color to amethyst, and 18 percent said that they would change their eye color to blue. After blue, turquoise came in fourth place, with 13 percent opting for that color, followed by gray (7 percent), honey (5 percent), and brown (4 percent).

Research also reveals that people with blue eyes are more demanding of eye contact than people with brown eyes. It is quite easy for us to look at a person with blue eyes and see the size of their pupils. When they expand and contract, it is evident. The person with blue eyes is used to people looking at him/her for an extended amount of time, in part because of the contrast between their blue eyes and black pupils. The contrast can be striking at an unconscious level.

People with brown eyes on the other hand are used to other people looking away more rapidly because at the unconscious level it appears that the person with brown eyes is not as interested in them! The brown eyes present a weaker contrast to the black pupils. It often appears at the unconscious level that those brown eyes are not interested in us! Therefore we tend to look away from the person with brown eyes, when in fact they may have been very interested in what we are saying!

When the person you are communicating with has brown eyes you must pay more attention to the eyes to see the contrast between the black and the brown. What seemed to be an uninterested person may be someone who is actually quite interested in you and what you are saying!

Confirming our beliefs about the value of eye contact in attraction is a study done some years ago. People watched films of a couple that communicated with each other in two distinct ways. The first film showed a couple that had eye contact during 80 percent of their communication. The second film showed a couple that had eye contact 15 percent of the time. The observers of the films rated the couples that had eye contact 15 percent of the time as cold, cautious, submissive, evasive, defensive, and immature (among others). The observers of the films whose couples had eye contact 80 percent of the time described the people in the film as mature, friendly, self-confident, sincere, and natural.

THE EYES DON'T LIE

Whenever you are in a situation where attraction takes place, there is plenty of room for deception! People have been known to stretch the truth about their age and income, their intentions, and even their degree of love for another. The eyes act as a leading indicator of truth and deception.

In 1997 and 1998 I was heard on hundreds of radio shows talking about the body language of President Clinton, Monica Lewinsky, Kathleen Willey, Hillary Clinton, and numerous other key players in the White House scandal that led to the President's impeachment. The interviewers wanted to know who was telling the truth, who was lying, and what the facts were based on the body-language cues I was reading.

Having carefully watched this President for almost seven years, I was familiar with his every facial expression and body posture. President Clinton certainly was the most charismatic president since John Kennedy. His ability to excite an audience and win over people who disagreed with him is legendary. He is an outstanding speaker who thrives on being in the limelight.

There were however two speeches and the famous grand jury testimony where the President was not his usual charismatic self. On these three occasions he was uncomfortable about the deception he involved himself in. The first was when he shook his right finger at the world and said, "I did not have sex with that woman, Monica Lewinsky." The next was during the grand jury testimony, where he was videotaped from the White House. The third was the speech he gave that very evening, after the grand jury testimony, when he offered his regret for being involved in the situation.

On these three occasions his eyes gave him away as being deceptive. The one speech that I want to share information with you about is the speech in which he apologized for his behavior.

For seven years I watched the President communicate with the country, and even though he had been called "Slick Willie," his body language rarely indicated any internal discomfort with what he communicated to the public. In this particular "apology speech," however, his anxiety, fear, and deception cues were very high.

When I watch someone to see if they are being deceptive, I look to the eyes for important cues. I want to especially know how many "eye blinks" per minute a person experiences in contrast to when he is telling the truth. For seven years President Clinton's "eye blink" pattern was about seven to twelve blinks per minute. That is normal. During the "apology speech," however, his eye blinking was recorded at seventy per minute! What that means is that on some level the President was being deceptive in his communication.

Once eye irritants such as contact lenses and allergies are ruled out, the only internal experience that will cause eyes to blink at that pace is the experience of anxiety normally associated with deception.

You should know that some people have eyes that

never blink, and a small number of people have eye tics that just won't stop blinking. On average, though, a person will blink from seven to fifteen times per minute. When a person is being deceptive, his eyes will blink five to twelve times that pace. Like pupil dilation, controlling one's eye blinks is very difficult if not impossible.

Take a moment right here and now. Simply try to keep your eyes open for thirty seconds without blinking. It's not easy, is it? Now here's another experiment for you: Stare at a friend for thirty seconds. No blinking is allowed.

It is very difficult to stop your eyes from blinking! If you are in conversation and someone is telling you about something, and suddenly you notice a big jump in the number of eye blinks per minute, you can safely bet there is some deceptive behavior going on somewhere in what that person is saying!

The eyes may or may not be the windows to the soul, but they certainly are strongly linked to the emotions and the entire makeup of the brain's responses to other people.

SOUND BYTES FROM SCIENTIFIC RESEARCH

- Generally speaking, the longer the eye contact between two people the greater the intimacy that is felt inside.

- Liking generally increases as mutual gazing increases.

- Others rarely interrupt two people engaged in a conversation if they have consistent eye contact.

- Pupils also enlarge when people are talking about things that bring them joy or happiness. They often contract when discussing issues that bring them sadness.

- Women are better nonverbal communicators than men. Men can improve though. One reason men aren't as good in reading body language is that men often communicate sitting or standing side by side and don't see as much nonverbal communication as women do.

- Women engage in more eye contact than men do.

- Eye contact has been shown to be a significant factor in the persuasion process.

- When women are engaged in a great degree of eye contact, they tend to be more self-disclosing about personal subjects.

- When eye contact decreases, men tend to disclose more and women tend to disclose less!

- The longer your eye contact, the more self-esteem you are perceived to have.

- The more eye contact you can maintain, the higher self-esteem you actually rate your self on!

You Never Get to Communicate if You Don't Make a Great Impression

Perhaps the greatest mistake of all is missing the opportunity to hit the radar screen of people you would like to communicate with. Perhaps the second greatest mistake would be to try to communicate with someone who has taken you off their radar screen because they just got a "bad feeling" about you.

Two seconds. That's it. That's about all you have to

make your first impression on another person. He/she will either be interested or not. You certainly can change that impression later *if* you get a further opportunity to do so. However, there will always be something in the back of their mind that remembers that first moment that they saw you.

That might be a good thing. They might have caught you performing a heroic act and will always remember that incident no matter what you do after that. Or they may have caught you at your worst, and you will have to overcome that impression, always trying to rectify that when they later learn things about you that are positive.

> *You have two to three seconds to impress a person.*
> *They will either like you or they won't.*

If you still are not convinced, go to the mall, to a bar, or to a restaurant. Look around at everyone there. How long do your eyes rest on that other person before you have made a judgment about them?

Are they attractive? Are they interesting? Are they worth the effort to possibly get to know them?

It doesn't take long to make that assessment, does it?

When you look around the room, what is it that really strikes you about a person? What is it that you notice first?

When scanning that room, how many of the people do you not even see? That may sound odd, but it's true. We have filters in our heads that actually filter people, objects, and events out of our minds.

It is like looking through a perforated shield. Some

of "reality" is completely blocked from vision. This is a convenience to the conscious mind as it narrows the decision-making process and relieves us of the effort. In our busy world there is just too much information coming at us in any given moment. If we had to try to consciously determine which of those events or objects to pay attention to in each and every moment, we would be exhausted and have no energy or brain space left over to do the things that we deem important.

Have you ever been out with a friend when they made reference to someone, only to find out that you didn't even realize that person was there? Before we even get to the phase of sorting who is interesting and who is not, an unconscious filtering system has already narrowed the field. People that are completely indistinct to us, or that offer no interesting possibilities, may be completely shut out of our field of vision. For teens, that may be middle-aged to elderly people, for instance. They may find "no use" for them, and therefore don't even see them consciously.

So our unconscious mind conveniently filters out the things that it has determined to be unnecessary at the moment. Of course, it could be wrong!

What is left for us to do is to look through the remaining holes in that perforated screen. We allow ourselves to pay attention to the narrowed field of vision. In doing so, we then begin the sorting process that tells us who is interesting and attractive and who is not.

Each of us has these filtering and sorting systems that we use to hone in on possible mates, potential friends, and people we want to be associated with. We will have different criteria for each of these categories.

If we are seeking out business associates, we will have a certain system of detecting who will offer a promising connection. We may be attracted to someone who appears to be self-confident, in control, and professional.

When we are making new friends, our sorting factors are different. We may be attracted to people who appear similar to ourselves. Those who exhibit similar tastes in clothes, hairstyle, hobbies and interests, marital status, and economic level would more likely come into view.

Yet when we are seeking out a romantic relationship, we have an entirely unique system of sorting. It is based on our past experiences, present conditions, and hopes and expectations for our future. Generally, when we are searching for the right mate or life partner, our guidelines become more specific and detailed.

> *Regardless of what those specific criteria are, the impression will be instantaneous. We filter out anyone who doesn't meet our unconscious standards.*

A man who has been "cleaned out" in a divorce, a businessman who has been ripped off by a partner, a woman who is coming out of an abusive relationship, or a teenager who is looking for his/her first love are all going to have individualized filtering systems. And as we move through life, our own criteria for sorting will change. As we mature, as we gain more experience, whether positive or negative, we adjust our assessment of what is beneficial and desirable to us and what needs to be avoided.

The First Glance: Prelude to Communication

The very first impressions will be based on the person's physical appearance and mannerisms. These would include clothing, hair, cleanliness, neatness, countenance, posture, facial features, weight, height, proportions, fitness, health, facial expressions, hand gestures, grace, and voice tone.

What strikes you first about a person will change as you look from one individual to another. You might notice one person because of her hair, while another person draws your attention based on the way she moves and smiles.

From our own perspective, we think we know everything that we need to know about a person from that first glance. It is highly discriminating, unconscious, and instantaneous. It is a natural, and actually an important, survival tool. Since the earliest days of mankind, it has been necessary to be able to instantly discern danger and tell the difference between friend and foe.

Without these discernment standards we would be attracted to everyone equally. Without our critical factors it would be as natural to be in love with Adolf Hitler as it would be with Princess Diana. Of course, this type of discernment should not be confused with generalized prejudices.

So we think that we know everything about a person from that first glance, but in truth we are probably quite off the mark. How many times have we dismissed a person or failed to be impressed until we got to know that person better? How often have we been amazed at our depth of fascination in another person—but not until a lengthier conversation? It happens all the time.

However, that's not the point. The point is that we, as humans, won't normally get that far if the initial attraction isn't there first.

It is true that a lot of relationships begin after a person has had numerous contacts with someone over a period of time. In these cases the person has had the opportunity to warm up to that other person based on something more than just the first glance. But we don't always have that opportunity. And, certainly, creating that scenario, and that opportunity, takes time, patience, and perseverance—things that, in our modern world, we don't always have a lot of!

So once again, the initial impression—that first glance—is so vitally important.

Wouldn't it just be simpler to start out on the right foot, with a great first impression? If your answer is "yes," you are primed for positive communication.

SAYING HELLO AND SHAKING HANDS

What should be the most natural thing in the world has become one of the most difficult. How do you say hello to your client?

Walk into the office with excellent posture taking medium-length strides and say, "Hi, I'm Kevin Hogan, author of *The Psychology of Persuasion*. You're John, right? Nice to meet you."

On the word "John," you shake hands. If you walk into the office and your client takes the lead by introducing himself, simply follow his lead and shake hands as he extends his.

Hold his hands for two or three beats and gently release it. Assuming you shake hands with your right hand, your left hand should NOT take part in this ritual. Here are the keys for shaking hands properly:

Nine Dos and Don'ts of Shaking Hands

✔ Always maintain eye contact when shaking hands.

✔ Do not use the infamous two-hand handshake.

✔ Do not grab his elbow with your left hand.

✔ Do not hold his hand for more than two seconds.

✔ Do not squeeze to crush his hand.

✔ Do not try to get a better grip than your client.

✔ Do not have a limp handshake.

✔ Your hand should be firm but under control.

✔ Your hand should be dry and warm.

Do You Walk Funny?

Many people walk funny. When I (KH) moved from the Chicago area to a small rural town in Minnesota in my senior year of high school, I learned this lesson the hard way. I had won a role in a play called "The Crucible" as the Reverend Mr. Hale. It was a wonderful role for the young person that I was. Unfortunately, I didn't walk "normally" and my posture was terrible. I had a bit of a "swagger" and my shoulders bounced as I walked. It was cute to some, but it was a sign of bad posture and needed correcting.

The drama's director, John Fogarty, needed his reverend to walk with an air of confidence and not a "Chicago shuffle." He decided he would tie five-pound weights to each of my ankles. Now that may not seem like a lot of weight but imagine a half-gallon of milk tied to each of your ankles. It slows you down and straightens you up. I had to wear these weights all day for six weeks. At the end of the six weeks I walked upright, not like the Cro-Magnon man I had come to resemble.

In life we all play roles. We play the roles of parents and spouses. We play the roles of volunteers and business people. As a salesperson, you play the most important role of all. You play the role of a person who literally helps the world go around.

When you are walking, you should be walking as if a big hand was scooting you along by putting pressure on your butt to go forward. This is an important first step to improved posture. Practice walking around the house as if a big hand was pushing you gently and slowly forward by scooting your butt forward. That will help you with your walk and your posture. The alternative is the weights . . . and that is a lot of work.

How Do I Communicate with Groups?

Everything you have read up until this point still applies, of course. Presentations simply offer a few more challenges and a few greater rewards.

If you are presenting to a group, you already know that you have something important enough to say to get the attention of the group. No one in the group showed up by accident.

Know what you are going to say in advance. You don't have to write out your presentation. In fact, unless you are the President of the United States, no one will listen if you do.

There are a few keys to speaking before groups. One is seat selection. If you are the key speaker and will be speaking from the one and only table, you want to sit on an end or in the middle of one of the two sides.

If you have any known detractors of your product or service, you should have them sit to your immediate left or immediate right. These are the least powerful positions at the table. Notice that in presidential press conferences where members of both parties were present at a seated table, President Clinton always had the house Republican leaders seated immediately next to him. These positions have no focal attention and rarely speak with any credibility.

If you have to speak before a group and you have a podium, you have an opportunity to make or break a sale by a strategy that I discovered by watching television evangelists. This strategy takes some time to master but is remarkably effective.

Communicate with Strategic Movement?

The most powerful nonverbal process you can use with an audience that must determine as a group to "buy" or "not buy" your products or services is that of strategic movement. Other sales trainers call similar strategies spatial anchoring. Both are applicable and here is what strategic movement is all about.

Do you remember Johnny Carson? He was the host of "The Tonight Show" for almost thirty years before Jay Leno took over in the 1990s. Each night when Johnny came out he stood on a small star marking exactly where he was supposed to stand. It was the best spot on the entire stage for camera angles and connecting with the audience.

Because of the curtain backdrop, we knew without seeing Johnny's face that he was there and not a guest host, who would stand on a different star.

The only thing Johnny ever did from this specific location was make people laugh. He didn't wander around the stage and tell his jokes. He stood right there and made people laugh. There were many nights when Johnny literally could just stand on his star and people would laugh. That is spatial anchoring. Audience laughter was anchored (conditioned to) Johnny's standing on his star.

When I (KH) first visited NBC in 1984, I thought it was fascinating that only Johnny stood on that star. At the time I thought it was an ego trip or some bit of arrogance on the part of Carson. How wrong I was. I knew nothing at that time of spatial anchoring and strategic movement.

When you are called on to make your sales presentation in front of a group, you are on stage. You are the star. You will want to select three specific points on the stage, or in the meeting room, from which to speak. Each of these points is a specific location and not an approximate area. Point "A" is your podium. Podiums and lecterns are used by teachers and preachers. Therefore *the podium (point "A") will always be used only to relay factual information to your audience.*

You will choose a point to your left about four feet from your podium that you will stand on to deliver all of the bad news discussed in your presentation. (You can't make many sales without painting a vivid picture about how bad things will get if the corporation doesn't hire you.) The bad news point is point "B," and you will only talk about problems and anything that is going to be perceived as "bad" by your audience. *Point "B" will be approximately four feet to the left of the podium.*

Point "C" will be approximately two and one half feet to the right of the podium, and you will always paint uplifting, positive, exciting, motivating pictures from this location. Everything we want the audience to agree with will be discussed from this point after we establish this as the "good news point."

Imagine that you are giving your presentation to this group and you need to be very persuasive. My favorite example here is that of fundraising for a charity. Your job? Get a big check for your favorite charity.

You place your folder or notes on the podium and immediately walk to "B" point. You tell a story about a hurting child or a suffering individual. You then explain how this one incidence is far from isolated. You move to the podium. You expound the facts and figures about the devastation of the problem that you are asking the group to help solve by making a big donation.

Now you move to point "C," where you will become excited about how the charitable organization is currently solving the problems and helping the suffering you talked about at "B." Everything that is good and wonderful you will "anchor" into point "C."

As you conclude your speech you will have a path that you have laid. You have moved from A to B to C to B to A, several times. **You conclude on point "C" because it is the good news point and offers each person the opportunity to participate in healing the wounds you opened at "B."**

The truly unique tactic in strategic movement is the ability to subtly answer questions at the unconscious level without saying anything significant on the conscious level. Imagine that the audience is given the opportunity for questions and answers with you. An individual in the audience asks you about the group's considerations of donating to a competing charitable organization.

"Well, of course, you know that charity is a good charity and there would be nothing wrong with that . . . of course . . . (walking to point "C") by taking advantage of the plan that we have, we can accomplish all of the goals that you want to have accomplished in the community. I'm sure you realize it is up to you to make it happen. We can only help those who need it if you make a decision tonight."

Discussing the other charity in a neutral or slightly positive manner from point "B" allows you to unconsciously associate all of the negative feelings with your "competitor" and you solve the problem as you move to the "C" point. *If you find this manipulative, then you are working for the wrong charity. If anyone else is more qualified to help a group, sells a better product, or offers a better service, you should be working for them!*

There is no more powerful manner of utilizing space than that of spatial anchoring and then using strategic movement. The next time you watch a great speaker, notice how he or she utilizes strategic movement. If they stay at the podium, notice how all the good news is given while gesturing with hand "A" and all the bad news is discussed when gesturing with the other hand. The greatest speakers are masters of spatial anchoring and strategic movement.

Communicate with Body Language

✔ The right side is where you make the best impression.

✔ Pupils dilate when they are interested in what they see.

✔ Rapid eye blinks often mean anxiety and deception.

✔ Forward leaning is a sign of liking.

✔ Eye contact when it isn't necessary is almost always a good sign.

✔ 70 percent eye contact is just about right in the United States.

✔ Your body weight sends a message.

✔ Your hairstyle speaks volumes.

✔ Hairpieces usually indicate insecurity.

✔ Rapport begins by matching physiology.

✔ Women feel comfortable when men are just a bit below eye level.

✔ Women feel comfortable when you are straight across from them.

✔ Men feel comfortable when you are at a 90-degree angle from them.

✔ Touch is a sign of liking.

✔ Nod your head. It unconsciously affirms your client.

✔ Look out for leakage, a sure sign of nervousness.

✔ The nose usually engorges when the person is deceptive.

✔ Dress appropriate to the situation.

✔ Radical dress means the person is making a statement. What?

✔ Spatial anchoring is a powerful nonverbal communication tool.

✔ The people who sit in Mom and Dad's chairs are looked to for assurance.

✔ The person sitting next to the person standing up has no power.

✔ People in rapport tend to synchronize together.

✔ Physical attractiveness means more than we wish it would.

✔ Blue-eyed people expect to be looked at more than others.

✔ Scents of vanilla are considered positive in the United States.

✔ Our face value goes up with each exposure!

✔ Negative emotions are usually triggered on the right side of the brain.

✔ Smile. It's tough to resist a sincere smile.

Remember, nonverbal communication makes up approximately two-thirds of all communication. Follow the simple tips in this chapter and your verbal communication will be richer and more meaningful.

Chapter Eight

Ignoring the Cycle
of Effective Communication

Men think differently from women.

It's that whole Mars/Venus thing. Any man who has ever tried to figure out what women *really* want knows this to be true. It seems to most men that women make the rules and every time men get close to understanding those rules, the rules get changed.

Any woman that has tried to understand why men never seem to grow up past the little boy stage also know this to be true. Women understand that for a man to be excited about something, it has to be loud, fast, and red. Just like those little toy cars that we used to push around the floor going Varoooooooom. Men just get bigger, louder, more expensive toys as we grow older.

Day after day, men and women interact with each other socially, professionally, and intimately and sometime during that day many have walked away, shaking their heads, trying to decipher exactly what the other party just said or what went wrong in the conversation between them. Exactly what happened? And how DID it happen?

It happened because very few of us recognize and understand the cycle of communication between men and women. We may share the same language but definitely not the same communication patterns. Sometimes, even when we do understand these patterns, we ignore them. Most psychotherapists agree that if people communicated better, there would be fewer emotional and psychological problems. Most people try to be interesting when they should be interested.

I've spent countless hours researching what works in communication. I've read books, listened to lectures, poured over research material, interviewed people involved in successful relationships, done my homework, and have found one thing that happens consistently.

No matter how much we learn, we still have to practice what we preach.

Just this morning I (RS) was working on a project with my youngest daughter. We were engrossed in attempting to fit together 5,000 pieces of a puzzle. My wife came in where we were working excited about something she had read that she wanted to share with me.

Now, if *you* have ever tried to put together one of those puzzles, you know 5,000 pieces is A LOT of pieces.

My dear wife was explaining this new theory and concept that she had just read as I was searching the table, trying to find pieces to the puzzle, attempting in vain to fit them together and listen to her. Only I wasn't listening 100 percent. Probably not even 50 percent.

It wasn't fair to my wife to shut her out like that, and I knew it was wrong, but somehow, beyond my immediate comprehension, my brain, muddled and overwhelmed by the sight of 5,000 puzzle pieces, still did it. Why? Funny, that was the same thing she asked me . . .

One of the reasons people fail in communicating with each other is they fail to fully understand what the other party *wants* before they try to be understood. Just as in the example of the puzzle above, I failed to understand the importance of what my wife was attempting to tell me and by the time I did, it was too late to repair the damage that had been done. The cycle of being ignored began: anger, rejection, and hurt feelings had set in, and I never have found out what was so important that she had to tell me.

Hearing someone instead of listening to them and failing to understand what is being said before trying to make your point are both conversation/relationship killers.

A good way to avoid this is to directly focus on the person speaking, setting aside whatever you are doing and listening. Giving that person all your attention, making him or her the most important star in the universe for as long as they are speaking. Then, after they are through speaking, paraphrase what they have said to make sure that their point has been fully understood by you.

Example:

"I read this interesting article that said the cycles of the moon can effect our behaviors."

"Really? let me put this puzzle piece down and tell me about it. There we go. So, it said that the moon could really control our mood and behavior?"

In this day and age, the term "multi-tasking," or

doing ten things at once, has become our nation's buzzword for the decade. In reality, it's simply impossible to do.

The human mind isn't capable of holding two thoughts simultaneously and becomes disoriented, disassociating from each of them. Because our minds process information so fast (some research has shown speeds of over one million bytes of information per second), it's easy to think we can do many things at once, such as listen to your wife while putting together a puzzle. The reality is that while we can do many things, we do many things *one* at a time.

Undivided attention is the **only** way to harmony in relationships.

> *When you make others feel special, they will realize how special you are.*

Can you read someone else's mind? I can't and probably neither can you. Most of us weren't born with this psychic ability. Then why do we expect our partners and spouses to do this, then become upset and angry with them when they can't perform this amazing feat either?

Another large piece in the communication puzzle is not asking for what you want.

Even more dangerous to a relationship is not asking for what you want and expecting the other person to *"know"* anyway.

If I had a dollar for every person who has come into my therapy office and told me that if only their wife, husband, kids, or parents had just *told* them what they needed from them, they might have still have a relationship, then I would be a rich man right now.

We are taught from childhood that it's wrong to ask for what we want. Most parents, at one time or another, upon entering a store have looked their children in the eye and told them, *"Don't even think about asking for something. The answer is NO!"*

As it is reinforced over time, that embedded command sticks with us through childhood and into adulthood. Those commands not to ask for anything don't have to be verbal but can be nonverbal as well.

Here's an example:

Our parents take us to a friend's house and there is a candy bowl sitting on the coffee table, overflowing with mouth-watering delights.

We want a piece of candy from that bowl. We begin to ask for what we desire, the candy, and get that "look" from our mother that we all too well know the meaning of. We become certain that there must be a conspiracy between parents of small children to place mouth-watering bowls of candy on coffee tables just to get little kids into trouble.

Mom gave us that "look" because she didn't want our sticky little kid fingerprints all over her best friend's freshly polished coffee table, not because she was part of a parental conspiracy.

But because of the fact we all had the same basic model of mom, many of us can't and don't ask for what we desire. Oh, we might drop hints: *"Wow, that would really look nice on me, and it's on sale, too!"* We leave magazines open to a certain page, circled in red ink to show what we want, in hopes that our spouses "read" our minds, and then we become very frustrated when they don't.

They must not love us anymore, the magic has left the relationship, we think, when the reality is that our spouses, our partners, are not superhuman beings with mind-reading capabilities. They are simply normal! Instead of going through all the drama of mind-reading, wouldn't it be much easier to express exactly what we want in the first place?

You would think so, but actually doing it is another thing. We could be rejected, judged, or criticized. Our spouses, friends, and partners could think we are weird or perverted if we stated our desires or our ideas.

How do we talk about sex with our spouse or significant other? How do we talk about religion with the relatives? How do we talk politics with our friends? How do we communicate with those we love in an honest way and STILL keep the relationship intact? It isn't easy but it can be done.

We must first establish a safe place for the sharing of ideas. One way is to allow your partner to share his/her ideas with you without fear of being judged, criticized, or rejected. They must know that whatever they tell you will be heard honestly and discussed as *possibility*. This doesn't mean that they have to receive everything they ask for, nor will you either, but each will gain a forum for a free exchange of ideas without fear of reprisal.

If your partner or significant other feels safe sharing *their innermost thoughts and desires,* it allows a doorway to be opened for you to share yours. It creates a Win/Win situation for communication.

> *Create a safe environment for desires. Plant the seeds of possibility. Water them by asking for what you want.*

Three of the sixteen basic desires that we humans all share is the need to compete, the need to seek power, and the need to seek status. These are hardwired into our brains from evolutionary time. These desires can manifest themselves in our conversation and communication patterns without our knowing or recognizing them.

Adding another piece to our communication puzzle is the need to "one-up" or become more powerful and compete with each other.

Generally speaking, women tend to see other adult women as peers, and prefer to treat one another as such. They gather for coffee or to "talk." It's kind of a women's club that men aren't privy to. While women may be intimidated by another's position of authority, they generally see others as equal. They are often baffled by the behavior of men toward them and toward one another.

While it's true that some men don't fit this category, far too many males simply cannot see any two people as equals. One of them must be superior and the other inferior. Every relationship, personal or business, is a battle to be king of the hill or to maintain the top spot. *"I'm smarter, more successful, richer, more knowledgeable, better looking than you are. And I'll do my best to prove it to you so we can both agree that I am one-up."*

They parade around, posturing and challenging other males to prove their virility in hopes that there are females watching. Watch any animal in the world. Typically, the male will try to outdo the other male with displays of plumage, fancy mating dances, vocal displays, etc. to prove who should be the one to mate with the female of the species. Most males are very simple creatures, driven by their libido and distracted by their left brain when the desires of their libido are not being met. Men don't have exclusive rights to oneupmanship but seem to practice it more.

I went to a comedy club with a male friend of mine one evening and was watching a comic do his act. My friend and I had seen this particular comic on television many times and we both knew his act by heart. Every time he came to the punch line of a story, my friend (who had drunk far too much) would yell out the line and spoil the delivery, stealing the spotlight and ruining the story for the comic. About the third time this happened the comic simply shot back, *"Listen buddy, I don't take the French fries out of your mouth when you're working."*

Amazingly, my friend was quiet from then on.

Listen fully before telling a similar story. Don't try to outdo or "one-up" the narrator by invalidating his story with an experience of your own. If you do, what you are really telling him is *"I'm not listening to you at all, but what I have to say is really important."*

Example:

"My last customer was the absolute worst!"

"He wasn't anything! My customer was unbelievable. He couldn't figure out that King Mac sauce didn't come with a filet-o-fish."

"Oh yeah, this one lady decided to just go off on me, cussed me like a sailor on leave just because the fries weren't crisp enough." ·

"That's nothing. This one customer took fifteen minutes and then finally decided to order a cheeseburger without cheese . . . and hamburgers were on special for 29 cents. Then he takes five minutes to get exact change . . ."

When you outdo someone, invalidate his story, you close off communication and rapport. The person you are communicating with subconsciously hears that you aren't interested in him or his experience. It is frustrating to be telling about a point of interest and have your listener respond with something similar that happened to him, effectively taking the attention away and stealing the spotlight. Make a special point starting right now of suppressing your own story when someone is talking.

> *Let the person sharing his story have his moment in the spotlight.*

Gaining clarity and closure before moving on provides a final piece of our puzzle in any segment or cycle of communication. It's the ability to acknowledge and confirm that what you said was understood and that you understood what was said to you in return. It's also the time to thank the other person for his views and input to the conversation.

You have probably sometime in your life been on

both ends of a communication or conversation that didn't "end." Someone you cared about walked out of a room, hung up the phone, or their cell phone cut out while they were speaking. They might have shut down in the middle on a conversation and switched subjects without explaining why.

If you felt angry or frustrated when the cycle of communication wasn't completed, congratulations! You're NORMAL!

Typically, when conversations aren't completed and the communication cycle doesn't go full circle, it leaves the person feeling confused, frustrated, and often angry because of the lack of completion. We want to hear the rest of the story.

By acknowledging that you have heard and understood what a person has said to you, you can always be certain to provide closure. This isn't meant to imply that you each must agree on everything; you can always agree to disagree, for example, but it is necessary to close each cycle of communication.

How important is closing the cycle of communication?

Think of a time in your life while during a conversation someone hung up the phone on you either in anger or without saying goodbye. How did it make you feel?

Think of a time that you did a special favor for someone, helped him or her move their belongings or bought them a gift, and they didn't say "Thank you" or express any appreciation or gratitude to you. How did that make you feel?

Think of a time when you were trying to explain a point and the other person walked out of the room, ignoring you. How did you feel?

Now ask yourself how important is closure to you? What specific actions can you begin to implement right now to prevent others from feeling that way about you?

> *Treat people as you would like them to treat you.*
> *Provide closure.*

Communicating with the people around us is something that we do every day of our lives. It's a fundamental and necessary function of surviving in the world in which we live.

By realizing the patterns and differences in men and women, recognizing the cycle of communication, speaking powerfully and purposely, and not just reading but *using* the tips explained in this book, you will grow in skill as a communicator and better avoid the common pitfalls as you forge long-term relationships.

Bibliography

Carnegie, Dale. *How to Win Friends and Influence People*. 1936. Reprint. New York: Pocket Books, 1990.

Eggerichs, Emerson E., Ph.D. *The Crazy Cycle*. http://www.loveandrespect.com/Articles/article.asp?aid=170

Fripp, Patricia. *Criticism: Bash or Boost? Turning Gripes into Growth*. http://www.fripp.com/art.criticism.html

Gottman John, and Silver Nan. *The Seven Principles for Making Marriage Work*. New York. Crown Publishing Group, 1999.

Gottman John M., and Silver Nan. *Why Marriages Succeed or Fail: And How You Can Make Yours Last*. New York. Fireside Publishing, 1995.

Gottman John, and Gonso Jonni, Notarius Clifford. *A Couple's Guide to Communication*. New York. Research Press, 1979.

Goulet, Tag. *Why Bosses Should Avoid Criticizing Employees*. http://www.fabjob.com/tips8.html

Hogan, Kevin. *The Psychology of Persuasion*. Gretna, Louisiana: Pelican Publishing, 1996.

Hogan, Kevin. *Selling Yourself to Others*. Gretna, Louisiana: Pelican Publishing, 2002.

Hogan, Kevin. *Talk Your Way to the Top*. Gretna, Louisiana: Pelican Publishing, 1999.

Hogan, Kevin. *Irresistible Attraction: Secrets of Personal Magnetism*. Network 3000 Publishing, 2000.

Imundo, Louis V. *The Effective Supervisor's Handbook*. New York. AMACOM 1993.

Kiersey, David. *Please Understand Me*. Del Mar, Calif.: Prometheus Nemesis Book Co., 1978.

Knapp, Mark and Judy Hall. *Nonverbal Communication in Human Interaction.* 3rd ed. Fort Worth: Harcourt Brace College Publications, 1992.

Leathers, Dale, *Successful Nonverbal Communication.* Needham Hts., MA, Allyn and Bacon, 1997.

Light, Harriett. "Dealing with Criticism." (June 1991). Paper presented at the pre-conference of the 82nd annual meeting of the American Home Economics Association, Minneapolis, MN. http://www.ext. nodak.edu/extpubs/yf/leaddev/he501w.htm

Kramer, Harriet J. Ph.D. *Relationship Killers: Part II.* http://singlestosoulmates.com/tlink/issuec7.html

MochaSofa. "Constructive Conflicts." http://www.mochasofa.ca/family/program/articles/01july09a.asp

North Dakota State University. Research Study, 1992. http://www.ext.nodak.edu/extpubs/yf/leaddev/he501w.htm

Peterson, Karen S. "Criticism pulls marital therapists asunder." *USA TODAY,* July 3, 1999. http://www.usatoday.com/life/health/family/marriage /lhfma029.htm

Promising Partnerships. "Strategies for Giving and Receiving Criticism Constructively." http://www.couples-place.com/qc005/toolbox.asp

Stubbs, Ronald. *Transformations: A Guide for Successful Hypnosis.* Island Publishing, 2001.

Sweet, Tabatha. "My Emotional Spin Cycle—The Four Options and the Two Bridges". http://www.soc.hawaii.edu/leonj/409bs2002/ sweet/report1.htm

Women Today Online. "12 Ways to Criticize Effectively. http://www.christianwomentoday.com/workplace/12waystocriticize.html

Need a Dynamic Speaker for Your Next Event?

Kevin Hogan, Psy.D, has presented his dynamic talks and energizing training programs about communication and persuasion skills all over the world. To receive a free information packet, call his office at (612) 616-0732. For further information about trainings and keynotes go to http://www.kevinhogan.net/